D1085144

SURPLUS - 1
LIBRARY OF CONGRESS
DUPLICATE

Real-Time Programming with Microcomputers

VANDERBILT UNIVERSITY

LIBRARY

NASHVILLE, TENNESSEE

QA
76.54
T87
c.3

Real-Time Programming with Microcomputers

Ronald C. Turner
American Sign and Indicator
Corporation

Lexington Books
D.C. Heath and Company
Lexington, Massachusetts
Toronto

Library of Congress Cataloging in Publication Data

Turner, Ronald C
    Real-time programming with microcomputers.

    Includes index.
    1. Real-time data processing. 2. Microcomputers—Programming.
I. Title.
QA76.54.T87   001.6'42   77-80773
ISBN 0-669-01666-7

Copyright © 1978 by D.C. Heath and Company.

All rights reserved. No part of this publication may be reproduced or transmitted in any form or by any means, electronic or mechanical, including photocopy, recording, or any information storage or retrieval system, without permission in writing from the publisher.

Published simultaneously in Canada.

Printed in the United States of America.

International Standard Book Number: 0-669-01666-7

Library of Congress Catalog Card Number: 77-80773

UNITED STATES AIR FORCE
AFGL Research Library

To my wife Audrey, and to Professors William Walden and Ottis Rechard, for recycling a Hispanist

And to Renn and Cameron, the first to ask why this book had to be written

Contents

ix

List of Figures

List of Tables

Preface

The most unfortunate misnomer in modern technology is the term *computer,* applied to the automated processing not only of numerical data but also of strings, logical operations, and infinite varieties of nonnumeric data structures. Running a close second is the lamentable terminological accident *software.* How the name suggested itself is evident. The catastrophic side effects of that term were destined to follow: *soft* means "easy" (doesn't it?), *flexible* implies "labor-free", *no wires* implies "no work." Printed circuit boards and hardware components cost money and visible effort; instructions taken from a manual or generated out of one's head are of only incidental cost, comprising only strokes on a keyboard or switch-setting on a front panel.

The central assumption of this book, amply documented in current literature, is that the development of software is a complex, costly area of real-time systems design. The software aspects of the design task constitute a technological no-man's-land at present. This lack of definition is manifested in several ways. Because of the relative adolescence of the software engineering discipline, there is no universally prescribed design methodology. Much, probably *most,* of the real-time software driving microcomputer-based systems today has been produced by hardware design engineers who profess little understanding of formal software design and coding technique. But if proper software techniques have been comprised to "make it run," the situation is not the fault of hardware engineers. For on the other side (the *far* side) of the no-man's-land, the applications programming community as a whole has remained ignorant of nearly all hardware considerations and thus has disqualified itself from any active role in real-time software development. True, cliché has it that it is easier for hardware designers to learn coding than for programmers to learn digital design, but in actual fact the practice of "coding to make it go" falls far short of well-engineered software (however embryonic the software discipline may be). As for the typical (data processing) programmer's crossing the "buffer zone," this possibility has continued to be remote at best. Nor does the standard university curriculum in computer science offer great hope. The only exposure to truly real-time computation in the student's computer science work has heretofore been in studies of operating systems, in which the process being controlled is the computer itself. The hardy computer science student who cross-registers in logic design and computer architecture courses in an electrical engineering department can at least hope to begin dialogue with the wider hardware design community. But even within real-time development groups, where one finds a healthy amount of *collective* expertise in both hardware and software design, it is often difficult for the two communities to share much common ground. The typical case is the climactic system integration phase of a project, in which both hardware and software designers naively assume that the *other* system will be totally functional from the very first. When that tandem illusion has been dispelled, the relationship may be characterized as one of light-hearted finger-pointing, rising tempers, mutual disdain, or outright hostility, depending on (1) the overall mental health of the group and (2) the number of hours of sleep gotten by each person the night before.

The preceding scenario, in which each camp is a separate and self-sufficient entity of knowledge, is more or less true in every developmental undertaking. But this state of affairs represents an unaffordable luxury. The spectacle of mutual cross-accusations by the two camps is not only lamentable and destructive of morale, it is costly—too costly to be allowed to continue. The most convincing argument in favor of cross-fertilization between software and hardware, however, lies in the nature of real-time programming itself. *Real time* implies "meaningful dialogue" between device and device, with software as a necessary intermediary. The key designers in any such system should ideally be neorenaissance types who are as much as possible at home in both camps. Not only will this enable systems design, implementation, and integration to proceed more efficiently, but the inevitable future maintenance of the system can be performed with equal smoothness.

This book therefore attempts to draw both parties into the exciting "buffer zone" of real-time software. It offers to the programmer an introduction to real-time concepts necessary for an awareness of what software should accomplish in conjunction with hardware. In particular, it introduces the architecture (barely) and instruction set (somewhat more amply) of the Intel 8080 micro-computer and then shows how that computer can be used in real-time applications. The hardware designer (who presumably has mastered the basic concepts of real-time processes) will gain an understanding and appreciation of sound practices in software design and coding as he views process control through the "eyes" of microcomputer code. Each constituency should benefit greatly from the study of tradeoffs inherent in both hardware and software. And the cause of real-world dialogue between the people in the two areas should be helped enormously by the attention given in the examples to interface structures used in the software (i.e., how programs "know" what is going on in a device at any given moment).

Basically, then, this is a book for and about *communication*—communication between designer and microcomputer, between microcomputer and external device, and particularly between designer and designer.

Not long ago, the world mourned the loss of 500 lives in a runway collision between two jumbo jets. We may never know for certain who was really to blame, but the ultimate cause of the tragedy was a failure in communication. Native technicians from three nations were attempting to coordinate the movement of independent, multimillion dollar systems involving hundreds of lives, and someone (perhaps two people or more) got the wrong message.

As more and more industries enter the high-technology domain, the development of large and sophisticated systems is forcing technicians together in ways even more heterogeneous than if they were of different nationalities. The "native languages" spoken by hardware and software designers differ to a far greater degree than did the differing accents of English spoken by the pilots and ground control on that fateful day in 1977. Fortunately, electronic systems design teams do not always deal in areas involving high risk to life, but they frequently are in control of design and production budgets involving millions of dollars and many man-years of effort. The technological world can ill afford the "luxury" of provincial dialects spoken by separate technical communities. What is needed is a bridge whereby technicians from both specialities can move more or less freely into each other's areas. The microcomputer may prove ultimately to be just that bridge. Hardware designers can now relate hardware components directly to assembler-level computer instructions, and software engineers can (and must) associate instructions with specific hardware building blocks. In the history of science written for this century, it may well happen that the microcomputer will be most remembered and esteemed, not for its *economic* effect (as revolutionary as that will have been), but for its secondary effect in reuniting the "two cultures" of hardware and software.

Within 10 years, perhaps much sooner, the "no-man's-land" we have described will in fact be a densely populated area of activity, and books of this sort will be museum pieces. Hardware, software, and firmware will have blended into a single new entity which one design engineer has inelegantly called "mushware." It is my hope that this book and the many books like it will help ease the growing pains of progress toward that new day.

All the clichés regarding "invaluable assistance and helpful criticism" were never more true than for this book. There is something inherent in computer systems that keeps one humble, constantly aware of one's error-proneness, lack of knowledge, and dependence on others. To the engineers in both the software and electronics design groups of American Sign and Indicator I offer my deepest gratitude. In particular, my thanks to Mr. Randy Bolster for insights from the perspective of electronic hardware, and to Mr. Don Harding, who wrote the PL/M example in Appendix C. Finally I must acknowledge the incredible role of the computerized text-formatting program at my disposal, which prepared countless versions of these chapters in a few seconds' time.

Introduction

The terms *real time* and *microcomputer* imply whole universes of intense activity in the electronics world. And any book with both those terms in its title would seem to promise a very lengthy and profound treatment of each. Nevertheless, this is a short book, and it has been kept brief for two very important reasons.

1. Its purpose is *not* to replace the programming language manuals supplied by hardware manufacturers. Its purpose *is* to impart sufficient basic knowledge to the designer/programmer that he or she can consult the appropriate manual in an intelligent and efficient manner. A programmer's manual (unlike a textbook) is *legalistic* in the sense that we typically refer to the manual to see whether the designer of the computer language has promised that a certain instruction will operate on our data in a certain fashion or to ascertain whether dire consequences will result from having used some instruction in a certain manner. Everyone agrees that manuals are not the best means of learning about a computer system, especially if one is studying one's first system for the first time. If we wished to become enlightened on the legal aspects of buying, holding, and selling real estate, we would welcome a brochure or pamphlet on the subject, or even a pertinent, clearly written chapter in a textbook on law or real estate. Only a very robust curiosity would prompt one to comb through the actual legal statutes on record with the state legislature. The purpose of the pamphlet or textbook is to *teach;* the job of the manual (as well as that of the legal record, believe it or not) is to *clarify*, using language that is as totally unambiguous as possible. This is often at the expense of readability, however.

2. This book's area of concern is a particular segment of the total applications activity that is possible with the microcomputer: real-time monitoring and control of external devices. As shall be discussed later, the actual *quantity* of code doing this type of work in a typical microcomputer system may be relatively small. More code may be used for performing the so-called housekeeping or background functions of the system. This is probably what some writers are thinking of when they say that programming a microcomputer is not essentially different from any other programming. The thesis of this book is that the portion of software design and development dedicated to real-time activity of systems *is* very different from other programming activities. That focus has therefore helped to exclude deliberately several of the topics found in most programming language textbooks.

Following, therefore, is a partial list of topics that will not be dealt with in this book:

Clever programming techniques. The activity now known as software engineering strongly emphasizes long-term productivity by designer/programmers. That is, a software package must not only be produced in a timely fashion, but it must also be modifiable (many people use the term *maintainable*) by the original programmer, by other software engineers, and by production people. (The interest in software on the part of the latter is to modify the original code to run some device that differs only slightly from the original device for which the package was designed.) An impressario who confounds the software world by compressing five pages of programming logic into a three-line macro may satisfy his own ego and may possibly gain some immediate admiration from his peers, but unless the code is easy to read and modify by someone other than the impressario (who will surely have moved on to broader horizons by the time the code needs revision), then more eventual harm may have been done to the total project than even a mediocre coder could have done.

Another salient characteristic of software engineering effort is that it is accomplished best by teams. The team may number only two, and one member may be pulled frequently from the project to do other tasks, but the code designed and implemented will always represent a team effort. And the principle of least effort assures that the "clever" code (which most often is obscure and difficult to grasp intuitively) never makes it beyond the consensus of the team. Only if some constraint demands that a certain routine be coded in a very "tight" (and possibly unreadable) manner should the team allow such code to see the light of day. And in such an exceptional case, the comments and other means of documentation should compensate for any readability difficulties of the code.

Arithmetic processing and number conversions. This is an important sort of activity that one encounters when programming in any assembler language. It is normally not the type of task performed in the real-time segments of a system, however. The only portions of this text touching on these activities will be in the discussions of data allocation and subtraction as performed in logical compares.

Specifications of individual instructions. In microcomputer systems it is extremely important to be aware of the time required for executing each instruction. And this is precisely the sort of information that is best consulted in the manufacturers' manuals. This book will deal primarily with instructions in the register-transfer sense: where the data originates, how it is moved or manipulated, and where it lands.

Macro writing. The topic of user-written macros typically constitutes the culminating experience in a course on assembler coding. And while macro capability is available in the 8080 assembler, the topic is omitted from this text for the following reasons:

1. It is an advanced topic that is not really essential in programming for real-time applications.
2. Assuming that the programmer has chosen deliberately to write code in assembler, it is very possible that the choice was made in order to keep a close eye on individual instruction execution times. The concept of macros is motivated by a desire to move beyond the consideration of individual

assembler instructions. But if the programmer wishes to produce macros, the language manual demonstrates how.
3. Macros tend to bring out the best (and for our purposes, the worst) of cleverness in people. As for cleverness, reread the preceding stern admonition.

High-level languages. While it is true that roughly half the code currently written for microprocessors is written in assembler, the use of high-level languages in increasing, even for real-time applications, in which time is obviously a critical consideration. There are several classic arguments in favor of using high-level languages (ease of coding and debugging, enhanced readability, need for less external documentation), but we shall assume that the largest (single) group of designer/programmers will continue to code in assembler for some time to come. We should hasten to add that the argument of this book is that *all* the sound practices of good programming, including structured programming, can be implemented in assembler; we shall attempt to show how.

The single most popular high-level language designed for the 8080 family of microprocessors is PL/M, and an example of PL/M is included as Appendix C.

Hardware design considerations beyond the processor chip. An executive of a well-known semiconductor manufacturing company was reported to have told his marketing division that if anyone asked whether a certain LSI (large-scale integration, i.e., superminiaturized) component was being marketed by his company, to say yes, since it probably was or soon would be. The point is that there is virtually an infinite variety of means of configuring a microcomputer system, and the designer should keep abreast of new products and technological breakthroughs. It is certainly beyond the scope of this book to venture beyond the 8080 processor chip itself, although we shall refer to some rather standard means of implementing interrupt-driven logic with 8080-compatible interfacing devices.

Emulation of digital logic design. The traditional curriculum in electrical engineering has provided the student first with the capability to design (and sometimes build) systems based on clocks, shift registers, flip-flops, plus inverters and various logic gates. But no matter how comfortable the engineering student (or practicing professional) may feel with such designs, he or she should view the microcomputer as a radically different means of accomplishing the same ultimate end. Simply because the microcomputer is a powerful single-chip device, it should not be considered as a means only of packaging more logic into single circuit boards. Rather than trying to make the microcomputer "speak" with the traditional vocabulary of hardware design, designers must orient themselves to the full power and flexibility of software.

To summarize, this book is not a carefully balanced treatment of programming as a whole, since it favors the topics of most concern to real-time programmers. Second, it leans hard on the importance of a consistent engineering methodology for designing software systems. Some readers may feel that the detailed treatment of the "hidden subtraction," for example, is out of all proportion to other similar topics. It was the author's intention to discuss such topics in the context of day-to-day examples rather than under the traditional textbook headings.

While it is impossible to say definitively what comprises the ideal reading matter for a course in microprocessor programming, the author strongly suggests that the *Assembly Language Programming Manual* published by Intel Corporation be used as a reference source in conjunction with this book.

1

The Computer in Real-Time Systems

The *real* of real-time computing shares two important characteristics with pornographic literature: (1) nearly anyone acquainted with the medium can recognize it immediately, and (2) it is nearly impossible to define with formal rigor. What definitions do exist are either too restrictive, too inclusive, circular, or not definitions at all. Normally, one finds *real time* "defined" by recourse to lists of attributes or characteristics. Shortly, we shall offer what may be the worst of all "definitions" to appear thus far: a narrow, nontheoretical working discussion of the phenomenon as applied only to microprocessors.

But first some preliminary observations. Whenever one hears the term *real* in *real time,* one suspects that this sort of computing contrasts itself to systems in which the time involved is in some sense less real (maybe even *unreal*), fictitious, phony, artificial, counterfeit, or the like. This, in turn, may imply to some that the programming done for real-time systems is also more genuine, more legitimate, or more substantial, and that other kinds of programming (whatever they may be) are considerably less than respectable. Worst of all, the practitioner of "real timery" may be tempted to use all this semantic underhandedness to intimidate the uninitiated.

If the preceding folk interpretations are 94 percent inaccurate, we must, in fairness, account for the 6 percent of truth they contain. The major premise of all real-time systems is that the domain of time totally within a computer (i.e., the ordering of its own instructions according to its internal clockery) is qualitatively different from the domain of time in the larger physical universe (whose "clock" is ultimately the sun's planetary system or, somewhat less ultimately, the time standard set by the U.S. Naval Observatory). In a non-real-time system, the computer can ignore almost completely the larger, "more real" world while it goes about its own tasks, generating payroll checks and associated records, for example. Naturally, there are real-time tasks at the systems level of any computer. A few of these tasks may be listed as follows:

1. Responding to input from the computer operator
2. Transferring data to and from mass storage devices
3. Outputting printable data to consoles and to hard-copy devices
4. Executing emergency procedures for unscheduled power-downs or momentary power "glitches"
5. Performing work-around procedures in the case of physical-device failures

1

But the applications programmer (a student submitting a job on punched cards, for example) using such a computer system (usually a very large and expensive one) can ignore the world of real time in the design of his or her system. The systems hardware and programming group must worry about the problems of the computer itself.

The real-time applications programmer, however, can never ignore the status or sequence of pertinent events in the larger universe. If the real-time program's task, for example, is to monitor atmospheric conditions and engine heat for the purpose of supplying a proper mix of fuel and air in an ignition system, the software must not simply "go away" once an initial mix has been established. The heat of the engine is going to fluctuate (dramatically when the engine is first started), and the program must constantly monitor the heat and readjust the fuel mix accordingly. This implies that the response to the input conditions must be timely. And this single characteristic (timeliness) of a real-time system is one that is found in every definition, weak or strong, theoretical or anecdotal, of real-time systems. All the definitions emphasize either the speed of the computer or at least the ability of the processor to "keep up with" the demands of the particular application. In a real-time system, time really is of the essence.

We have thus seen that *real* in *real time* is *more real* only in the sense that the universe to be considered by the programmer is larger—that it refers to *time* in the ordinary (time of day) sense.

Now we will offer our own working definition of a real-time system as used in this text and then comment on several of the more significant points of the definition. The *real-time segment of a microprocessor-based system* is that portion of the total system in which the computer's principal task is to monitor and/or control a time-critical process whose own logical sequence is asynchronous to that of the computer itself.

Let us now examine some implications of five of the terms used in the working definition of a real-time system.

Principal task. Our assumption is that a portion of the microprocessor's total time is dedicated to the monitor/control function(s) specified. Less than 10 years ago this assumption would have been unthinkable for all but life-and-death (or, for other reasons, well-funded) applications: missile tracking, monitoring of nuclear reactors, life support in medical systems, and speed and braking controls in mass transit systems, to cite but a few examples. With the cost of microprocessor chips now in the under $20 per unit range, it is everyday design practice to dedicate a computer's full power to such banal (but nonetheless interesting) applications as home TV games, hand and wrist calculators, automobile diagnostic systems, home kitchen microwave regulators, and programmable TV viewing schedulers. The story of real-time processing is mainly a story of dedicated processors, and the monumental growth of real-time activity is almost totally a function of the economics of the semiconductor industry.

Having just used such emphatic descriptors as *principal,* and *dedicated,* I must immediately qualify what this really means in a typical microprocessor system. *Dedication* here means that the computer's top priority is to service some external device. The actual code and execution time needed to perform that service can be miniscule compared to that of the total system. However, the task of servicing the external device will always be of top priority.

Monitor. In order for a computer to make something function properly it must of course gather sufficient facts to start, stop, slow down, or speed up activities at the proper times. This in turn implies that the controlling processor must spend some of its time inputting pertinent status information. And in certain applications, the computer may be meant only to monitor a process and not to take any action beyond reporting some device's status to the user. An automobile diagnostic system is an example of a monitor-only system. The mechanic connects an output device to the microprocessor in the automobile. The microprocessor in turn simply reports on specified parameters.

Control. The topic of control by computers is so central to real-time systems, as we are describing them, that many specialists would prefer to call this book a text on "process controls." (The two terms are in fact used almost interchangeably in employment advertisements.) Manufacturing engineers also use the term *numerical control,* although such systems may not fit our definition of real time.

At this juncture we must offer a rather refined distinction in order to account fairly for another whole area of real-time computing we have chosen to exclude from this discussion. This is the type of application in which the process to be controlled is not a device or mechanical process but instead is a dynamic data base. A typical example is an airlines reservation system whose data base is being queried (read from) constantly to determine free seats. The data base is also being written to with every new reservation, cancellation, or change in the details of an existing reservation. In the double sense that (1) the response time to such an inquiry is virtually immediate, and (2) that the "life" of the data base is somewhat separate from the logic of the interrogation algorithm, such a system can be said to be real-time. However, we are excluding such "real-time" systems on less theoretical grounds:

1. The "real-time" systems with which we are concerned are not data-base oriented.
2. The systems we are concerned with normally monitor or control, directly or indirectly, some other hardware device.

The first criterion is purely quantitative: process control can normally be done by mini- or microcomputers, while real-time access to very large data bases (which must reside on large, high-speed peripherals) demands a much larger computer system.

One example of a real-time application in the process-control sense is a programmable dicing saw used for cutting semiconductor wafers into chips, which later will be manufactured as the familiar large-scale integration (LSI) electronic chips used on printed circuit boards. The uncut wafers are expensive, and it is critical that the initial cutting or grazing be performed within microscopic tolerances. This particular product performs the required cutting automatically and precisely according to the parameters set by the operator.

The automatic control of tooling or cutting materials (hard or soft) is standard practice in many industries, although the tolerances may not be always as critical as for the LSI chips just mentioned.

The difference between the time domain of the real world and that of the computer may be very noticeable. Consider a microprocessor system for detecting excessive steam pressure level in a chamber. When the pressure reaches a certain level, a valve is opened, and it is opened further for each pound of pressure beyond the "opening level." There is nothing about a computer that makes it "conscious" of such phenomena as steam pressure and increases or decreases in steam pressure. The task of the hardware and software designers is to make the computer totally "aware" of these phenomena in such a manner that the computer's internal world of memory fetches, instruction cycles, and program execution will be all but transparent to the observer.

In other applications, particularly ones in which the computer is working at nearly full speed to "keep up" with an external device, the distinction between internal computer time and real time may be very much obscured. The case of the controller of an incandescent lamp bank display is a good example. One of the special effects of displaying a frame (i.e., a full matrix's worth of bit-image data) is to light the lamp bank column by column from left to right, the net effect being to reveal the picture as though a curtain were being drawn back. One method of achieving this effect, with minimal assistance from hardware, would be to add successive columns of bit-image data to an output buffer and then, after building each column, to refresh the lamp bank with the updated contents of the output buffer. In order to prevent jerkiness in this "curtain mode," the refresh rate must be smoothed to a set number of columns per second. For a very large lamp bank, such a system is constantly near to being compute-bound (i.e., CPU-bound, limited by the speed of the central processor). But even in this type of "superdedicated" system, in which the microprocessor appears to be intimately linked to the controlled device, we must recall that frame rates, display modes, and all the associated hardware of the lamp bank display "mean" nothing to the internal world of the microprocessor. Once again, it is up to the designer/programmer to make the two worlds talk to each other. (This task is the essence of hardware-software interfacing, and will be discussed in a separate chapter.

Time critical. In a "batch" system, found typically in university computing centers, the "response" by the computer to a user may be measured in hours, even in half-days during end-of-term peak periods. And even in the "real-time" reservation system mentioned earlier, the response time to the user may take up to several seconds. But the time constraints of the systems with which we are concerned here normally are in the order of fractions of seconds, probably in milliseconds or less.

Asynchronous. The concept of asynchronous events within a single system is familiar to hardware designers. Even within circuits of relatively simple design it is likely that pulses or voltage levels will travel through relatively independent portions of the circuitry and will exhibit highly independent timing patterns. In such systems it is normally imperative that asynchronous circuits ultimately be synchronized for the system to function properly. This is accomplished by means of a system clock (a crystal-controlled timing device with a known frequency, for example) that issues periodic pulses which are received by whatever components of the circuit need synchronization. Consider, for example, the design for a data input device consisting of two-state push buttons. Conceptually, it is tempting to envision the voltage level simply going high whenever the operator pushes the button and then returning to low when the button is released. But in order to assure both (1) that a very brief push is recognized by the system and (2) that a prolonged push does not disable the system, it is necessary to "latch" the input signal the instant it is received from the button. And once the signal is latched in the system, the button should be disabled internally so that prolonged pushing will have no effect on the system. The latched signal will then be held until the system is ready to process it in proper fashion. The precise moment that this latched signal will be "read" and processed will very likely be the next "tick" of the system clock. By this strategy the designer has assured that a "blind" piece of hardware can respond internally in an orderly manner to some randomly timed event in the external world.

Just as for any other electronic system, the major design task in real-time systems is to make the computer's logic totally responsive, as its first priority, to pertinent events in the monitored/controlled process. However, even though real-time matters may be the first priority of the processor, they are not its only responsibility. There are always "housekeeping chores" associated with the time-critical tasks, chores which themselves are not so time-critical as the control functions. For example, in order for the lamp bank display controller to know how to lay out a frame of image data, it must determine how many lamp points ("pixels") constitute a "column." It must then set the proper bits in some image buffer to ready the buffer for outputing its contents to the actual display. This sort of calculation and bit manipulation should be done totally apart from the time-critical portion of the system.

All this suggests that not only is the "raw" state of the computer (i.e., without interfacing software) asynchronous to the controlled device, but also that within the processor itself, when the software is functional, there will exist subsystems which themselves are asynchronous one to the other. There are "foreground" (highly time-critical) spheres of activity which service the real-time demands of the system. And there are "background" (less time-critical) tasks which use whatever processor time is available. Initializations, bookkeeping functions, and data structure manipulations are typical "background" activities.

If interfacing asynchronous machines is the major task of hardware and software designers working cooperatively, then the creation of asynchronous systems within the software itself is surely the central task of the software designer/programmer team. One of the keys to accomplishing such apparently complex software systems is *interrupt handling,* a strategy that is amply supported by the architecture and instruction set of the 8080 family of microprocessors. We shall be dealing with interrupt handling in careful detail in a later chapter.

We have thus far defined in a very anecdotal fashion a microprocessor real-time system. At this juncture it is only fair to point out that real-time systems that control asynchronous devices need not necessarily include a computer. In fact, for the reader with a basic knowledge of circuit design, the whole notion of monitoring and controlling an external device should sound very reminiscent of feedback control (or servo) systems (which do not necessarily incorporate a computer in their design). Since this is such a significant area of systems design, and since it is an area that has been invaded so decisively by the computer, it seems worthwhile to survey briefly the nature of feedback control systems.

Let us begin with an example that later can lead us easily to a general case. Consider a valve controlling an irrigation conduit. In the original nonautomatic, operator-attended design, the valve is controlled remotely such that it can be made to open (gradually), to close (gradually), or to remain at its current position. Since this particular conduit is but one of several in the total system which must be in use at the same time, it is critical that the rate of flow of the water be kept to within narrow tolerances. Too much flow locally would drop the pressure to an unacceptable level on the other lines, and too little would prevent adequate irrigation to the local sector of land. We can easily picture the overall operation of the valve control mechanism as in Figure 1-1a. In this case the input line to the local valve controller represents the variable voltage supplied from the central command station. The voltage level determines whether the valve is to continue opening, remain at its current position, or continue closing. The output line from the valve in this case is an analog signal to indicate to the operator the flow rate of the water, a signal that drives appropriate meters, which are read and interpreted by the operator. In order to reduce the amount of operator intervention necessary, as for the case of significant fluctuation of input pressure to the total system, it would be desirable to have the valves adjust themselves depending on the actual water pressure. Without involving ourselves in the details of implementing such a system, let us modify the block diagram as in Figure 1-1b. In this particular modification, the operator still maintains "manual" control over the valve, as before, and he will still be able to monitor the flow, but we now have included a feedback control loop in the total system.

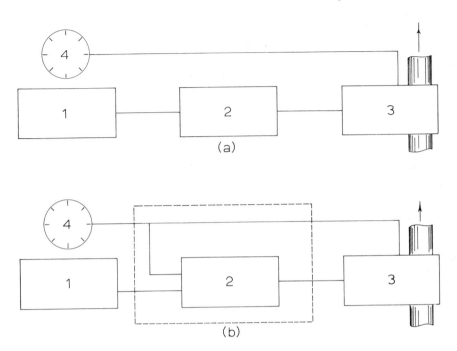

Note: The components are identified as follows: (1) operator input, (2) input amplifier and final controller, (3) water valve, and (4) flow rate indicator.

Figure 1-1. Irrigation Control System.

In this system, the rate of flow (and, for that matter, whatever other data are pertinent) is transmitted not only to the central command station but also to the servo system. To be a bit more formal, the output of the device to be controlled becomes an input to the controller. The controller interprets those data and then exerts real control over the main valve system. Let us assume, for the moment, that the controller is not a computer but instead consists of solid-state logic that is able to compare the input data against values received and interpreted by the translator mechanism. This controller then would issue appropriate commands to the valve control proper.

The most significant point for our purposes is the sequence of data exchanges between the controlled device and the feedback control device:

1. Receive data on the status of the controlled device (INPUT)
2. Interpret those data and make appropriate decisions (PROCESS)
3. Transmit the command information that corresponds to the decisions (OUTPUT)

It is precisely this sequence—input, process, output—which is so natural to a computer. And this affinity, in turn, leads designers to adopt a computer-based system whenever possible. If there is considerable decision making involved within the design, then a computer-based system is almost imperative. Let us examine a further revision of our irrigation system, this time incorporating a computer to implement all the functions contained within the dotted line in Figure 1-1b. The ever-decreasing costs of microprocessors are forcing the trade-off point between the cost of a microprocessor chip versus the cost of other types of chips to an ever decreasing number (much lower than 100 chips, as a rough estimate). Furthermore, everyone assumes that the software in a micro-computer system is easier to change than the logic designed from pure integrated circuit (IC) chip components. (The reader who eventually works in a true hard-ware/software interface environment will learn soon enough about the rampant debate over just how "easy" it is to change software.) Perhaps the only safe thing to say is that the software is at least more amenable to change. (We shall return to this issue later on in the text.) Finally, the designer must consider a hard economic fact of manufacturing that the cost of placing an IC chip on a circuit board is between $2 and $6 per chip, exclusive of the cost of materials, and regardless of the type of chip. In view of this sort of per-chip overhead cost in manufacturing, it is reasonable to select a chip with the greatest amount of decision-making capability whenever it is feasible to do so. A microcomputer is a natural candidate.

Our purpose in discussing feedback control design is not merely to appease the readers with a background in digital design. Instead, we are attempting to define more precisely what is meant by calling the microcomputer the "con-troller" or "master" in one particular type of real-time control system. One frequently hears the terms *master* and *slave* when referring to a computer and an external device (the device being controlled). We wish to make it plain to the electrical engineering types that even when this highly metaphoric terminology is used, the broad picture of the system is very similar to what they have worked with already in feedback control logic.

As for the reader with a heavier emphasis in computer science, this digres-sion was meant to provide a brief introduction to how "master" and "slave" devices function in such a system. Furthermore, we wish to make it clear that al-though the microcomputer provides much greater power and flexibility for decision making in a logic system, the programmer is doing in a more pliable medium basically what the hardware designer has been doing all along (at least in the case of feedback loop design). Now thanks to the greater flexibility of the medium (coded instructions versus printed circuits and specific chips), the programmer/designer can do it better.

In every real-time microcomputer system, the microprocessor is in control of at least one device. Since the particular applications of systems may differ so widely, it is a bit difficult to generalize about the nature of this control. In the case of the irrigation valve previously discussed, it is easy to conceptualize control over the process (ultimately) as actual, physical adjustment of the device; the valve orifice is increased or decreased in response to signals from the processor. A computer-controlled heating system for a refining furnace would be another very observable case of control by the computer. The initial input to the system from the operator specifies that a given temperature is to be attained within the furnace, and the computer initially determines through repeated samplings of the actual temperature of the furnace that more heat is needed. When the desired temperature is attained, the processor "decides" to discontinue adding new heat to the chamber until the moment that the heat once again drops below the threshold specified.

But there are ways of controlling the activity of external devices which do not alter either physical configuration or such tangible characteristics as temperature. Consider our case of the computer-controlled lamp bank display. True, the computer plays an active and vigorous role in deciding just which lightbulbs are to be turned on (and with what intensity, in a gray-scale system), but once the act of turning on the lamps has been accomplished, the computer does not "hang around" to monitor the display in the sense that the irrigation controller monitors the water flow or the refinery controller monitors the temperature of the furnace. Rather, the lamp bank controller acts merely as an "absentee timekeeper" to determine when the configuration of the lamp bank is to be altered. In the case of an animating display, the time involved may be only a small fraction of a second, but the processor is a mere timekeeper nevertheless. Thus the concept of "real-time control" applies not only to controlling "how much" or "how hot," but even to such properties of the process as "for how long."

It is important for the programmer of real-time control systems to feel something of the power that is inherent in the data structures and logic of the code ("firmware") he or she will write for the microcomputer. The entire decision-making process within the particular device controller will likely center around a very few bits of information: "I [the processor is speaking] see from bits m through n in the temperature indicator register that the desired level has not yet been attained. Therefore I shall continue to add more heat to the furnace by leaving bit p set in the high position." That single bit p may therefore ultimately result in a temperature of hundreds of degrees. The power that is left at the disposal of the programmer is made possible through the hardware, which essentially translates and amplifies firmware commands (even commands of a single bit in length) into the physical phenomena associated with the external device, e.g., heat, water flow, lamps on, lamps off.

The few essential bits within the memory of a controlling processor which control an external device are nearly always linked to that device in a very indirect manner. It would be physically impossible for the low-voltage change produced by changing a single bit in memory to open directly a large water valve. Rather, that bit change is sensed by a device which is external to the processor and which, in turn, begins the amplification process previously mentioned. Or in the case of the lamp bank controller, it would be impossible to hard wire 2000 bits of addressable memory directly to the individual sockets of the lamp bank. In such an application, the bit-image data are normally serialized through a single data line from the processor and then formatted at the sign itself for display. So here too there is a chain of events that is quite separate from the internal world of the microprocessor. All this leads us to observe that in every real-time microcomputer application the device being controlled is external to the processor and operates in a world that is totally its own. To be sure, the device is linked to the processor, but that link is indirect at best.

Whether a computer's central task is to calculate payroll records or to control the flow of gas in a heating plant, that computer is only capable of a limited repertoire of activities. These activities are well known to anyone with even limited programming experience; they can best be examined by reference to the instruction set of the machine's assembly language, e.g., moves, logical operations, and arithmetic operations, and some miscellaneous "extras" which may be peculiar to the particular machine. We mention this only because it is tempting for someone unfamiliar with real-time programming to suppose that when a computer is programmed to control a real-time task such as to regulate the flow of water there is a special set of real-time control instructions the programmer can draw upon, "compare pressure to specified maximum" or "close valve," for example. Except for a very limited number of "special" instructions, the programs written for real-time applications consist of code that appears to resemble the most typical batch-mode data processing operations: shifts, adds, subtracts, decrements, compares, branches, and jumps to subroutines, to mention a few. Simply because a microprocessor is controlling some task, it does not mysteriously "become familiar" with the task. The processor in itself does not become sensitive to heat and cold, to higher or lower pressure, nor does it become any more acutely aware of the passage of time than it does under non-real-time circumstances. Whether the microprocessor's board is located 2 centimeters or 500 kilometers from the external device it is controlling, that device is *external* to the computer. The entire burden for integrating the microprocessor into the overall system which it is to control is on the designers of the hardware and firmware that is to comprise the system.

Since the microcomputer's central task in a real-time system is to monitor and control an external device, and since that device is totally removed from the interior world of the processor, it is easy to conclude that the central task of the designer/programmer is input/output (I/O). And while it is true that we have insisted that the bulk of instructions used in any real-time system will probably resemble those used for any other application, we should note that the centrality of I/O operations is one important distinguishing characteristic of real-time programs. This is bad news for the reader with limited programming experience, particularly if that experience has been with a high-level language such as

FORTRAN, in which even to output a single line is little short of painful. And programmers with experience only on large machines with complex operating systems not only do not get the opportunity for much "hands-on" experience in genuine I/O with the various devices, but they must be *prevented* from such direct interaction or the system could easily be made inoperable for long periods of time. And the engineering specialist is perhaps at an even greater disadvantage because his or her exposure to programming has typically been in some "short course" that covered only the barest essentials of a selected programming language. The "essentials" for engineering students are usually assumed to be problems of encoding equations, using "canned" library programs, and manipulating arrays. Those who struggle with the typical "first course" in programming come away with the suspicion that the designers of programming languages have left all I/O considerations as "extra-credit exercises for the student."

The good news for everyone attempting to program the microprocessor for real-time applications is that I/O is integrally designed into the hardware and is therefore a nearly trivial operation, at least in the case of the 8080/8085. As was noted, the programmer must be fully aware of everything going on as data are moved in and out of the processor, unlike the situation of a patronizing operating system which shields the user from unnecessary complications. But the very visibility of every minute operation in microprocessor programming only helps to clarify matters.

To say that the central task of the real-time programmer is I/O with an external device is to say that the real-time programmer is in the communications business. (We are not referring to true computer-controlled communications systems, in which the ultimate process under the computer's control is communication.) For the designer/programmer of both hardware and software, this implies that the product requirements and final design specifications must be as tight and as firm as the hardware and software itself. It would be absurd for the hardware and software designers to work in isolation until each had completed what he "sincerely hoped" would be able to communicate with the other portion of the system. Instead, what must occur during the design phase of such a system is for each party to determine the sequence of communications exchanges between the devices (microprocessor and external device) and the semantics (content) of each data transmission. The narration of such a real-time exchange might be as follows:

1. The microprocessor will test to see if the device is ready (to perform whatever task is expected).
2. When the processor finds that the device is ready, then it will send the device the necessary data.
3. The device will respond that it has gotten the data and will report to the processor again when it is ready for more data.

The term used in communications for describing this sort of interchange is *protocol,* a term borrowed from the world of high-level diplomacy. There *protocol* refers to behavior that is totally defined prior to the occasion under consideration. A high official is briefed thoroughly by a chief of protocol as to how he should greet his official guests, e.g., bow, salute, kneel, wink, kiss the hand, doff the hat, remove the hat, embrace, shake hands, or none of the above. When the occasion finally takes place, the behavior is all predetermined. Protocol is the overriding force determining the external behavior of each party. The actual conversation that ensues will certainly be more spontaneous and less predictable. And so it is with protocol in real-time communication between a computer and its external device. The sequence and format of what is to be said is all predetermined by the system designers. The content of the exchanged data will be determined by events at the actual ("real") time the program is run.

But there is more to communication than the "when" and "in what order." In order for hardware components to "talk to each other" in the manner necessary in real-time systems, both parties must know precisely where the interchange is to take place. In the case of the hardware, this means that a certain pin on the processor chip or a given memory location is known by the entire system to be dedicated to a particular communications function. The software designer knows ahead of time precisely which word of memory will be used for the exchange and which bits within that word will be used to convey each portion of the messages. I/O therefore demands precise configuration assignments in order for the necessary communication to occur.

Although much data are moving into and out of a microcomputer during the running of a real-time system, it should provide some comfort to the reader to note the following rules:

1. All data moving from the device to the processor are ultimately for the purpose of reporting the *status* of the device.
2. All data moving from the microprocessor to the device are ultimately for the purpose of *controlling* the device.

This two part rule may seem to be a gross oversimplification, especially when we consider the topic of interrupts. But considering the system as a system, the microprocessor is the controller, and the device is controlled. Whenever a controlled device is allowed decision-making power of its own and thereby "breaks free" from the absolute control of the central processor, the system is doomed to failure. (This almost occurred during an exploratory trip to Mars, in which a spacecraft received certain commands but "refused" to act on them.) There is nothing democratic about a real-time system!

A further distinguishing characteristic of all real-time programs, which is obvious even to a novice reader of the code, is that the program at the main level (i.e., the code which may call subroutines but which itself is called by no higher-order routines) has no "end" or "exit" point. Typically, there is a labeled entry point in the code from which the program counter in the central processing unit commences execution of the program. But from then on (barring a crash and a subsequent restart), the program loops forever at this main level, dropping into certain subroutines (and interrupt service routines, as we shall see later) as events may dictate. For the graduate of the typical undergraduate programming course, the concept of looping forever carries only negative connotations. This aversion must be dispelled immediately.

Although it is difficult to characterize all real-time programs with a few brief generalizations, I can suggest the typical list of activities performed by a microprocessor in a real-time system, arranged by order of their priorities:

1. *Control the external device.* (We are not concerned here with what *control* implies, nor do we care what this particular "device" accomplishes.) The programmer must not simply *allow for* the microprocessor to monitor and control the external device. Rather, the entire design of the software must be focused on continual, timely service to the device. Whether the device needs servicing very frequently (as in the case of an interface to/from a remote data terminal) or very infrequently (as in the case of a heat-sensing alarm system), the response by the processor to the device must always be the top priority of the processor.

2. *Perform low-priority (background) tasks.* In many applications, the speed of the real-time device is such that the microprocessor can satisfactorily service the device and still have most of its time available for other tasks. The data interface mentioned earlier may need to service the communications line very frequently in order not to miss any of the signals addressed to that interface. However, on a slow-speed communications line (such as a voice-grade telephone line), this task may still leave the microprocessor interface with time enough to display the incoming characters on a CRT display, for example. In this case, the "external device" is the communications line, and the high-priority task is to receive and transmit characters over that line. The software designer's task is to determine precisely how much time is left over for low-priority tasks and then to structure the software so that such background work never interferes with the high-priority activity.

Not all "background" activity need be concerned with work related directly to the moment-by-moment operation of the system. As system maintenance becomes more and more significant, it is necessary to include diagnostic tools within the software. With the advent of nonvolatile RAM (random-access memory, a read/write memory that retains its state after power-down), it is possible to design system logging functions into the software. Such functions may include the following: total elapsed time that the system has been running, number of operations performed (whatever type of operation the device is to perform), number of total received messages (in the case of a communications interface), number of errors (parity errors in the communications system, for example).

In the case of the nonvolatile RAM, it would be possible to maintain a frequently updated *system snapshot*. This would essentially be a very dynamic "status report" depicting the state of every pertinent device in the system as well as the vital memory locations of the processor itself. A troubleshooter could thus trace problems more easily and more directly to the faulty components.

3. *Perform null tasks.* As was mentioned above, it is characteristic of real-time, event-driven software that there is no "end" or "exit" point within the main routine. But the processor must be kept running in order to service the device(s) properly. Quite often, therefore, the controller's software will simply execute a loop in the main routine, a loop that constitutes a "null task" to be performed whenever there is nothing else to do. Or the designer may wish to incorporate a "Hey, I'm alive!" function in the system in which the processor periodically causes some LED (light-emitting diode, a small light) to blink, indicating that the system is indeed running.

Exercises

1-1. Scan the employment pages of such publications as *Computerworld, Electronic Engineering Times,* and other technical periodicals, plus such major newspapers as the Sunday *New York Times* and *Los Angeles Times* to see which companies mention *real time* and/or *microprocessors* explicitly in their advertisements. Note the types of products and systems that are manufactured and serviced by these companies. Note especially the "buzz words" that typically appear in the same paragraphs with *real time.*

1-2. It is a commonplace saying among engineering groups that it is unwise, even counterproductive, to put a programmer with only data processing experience to work on a real-time development project. Do you see why this may be true? Can you suggest ways for students of computer programming to become more oriented to real-time systems as they are described in this chapter?

1-3. Describe five microprocessor-based systems in which the computer's main task is "merely" to monitor and not to control some external device. Be sure to pick applications that are within the capability of a microprocessor. (Monitoring power fluctuations from a large hydroelectric system would require more than a microprocessor.) Do not be concerned about economic feasibility or whether or not the product already exists.

1-4. Describe five possible systems to be used in manufacturing that might use a computer (up to mini-sized) in the "numerical control" sense.

1-5. Describe how the operating system of a typical large computer fits our definition of a real-time system, particularly the portion of the system concerned with peripheral devices (keyboards, printer, and card readers, for example).

1-6. In the discussion of the time criticality of real-time systems, we mentioned the turnaround time in university computing centers as being normally very long (in the order of hours). If the turnaround time were somehow shortened to 30 seconds or less between the time that a job is submitted and when it is returned to the user, could such a system then be called "real time?" (Such systems often include an "interactive task" portion of the operating system by which a user, typically at a teletype, can expect turnaround time in order of seconds.)

1-7. The example of an asynchronous system that was given in the text is a fair illustration for electronic systems. Try to think of an analogous asynchronous-then-synchronous system in the sociological sense. Think of separate social entities operating independent of one another but occasionally brought into "sync" by some special event. (In the electronics example, the tick of a clock built into the circuit was the "special event.")

1-8. Any good programmer knows (a) that all programs must terminate properly, and (b) that endless loops must not happen in properly designed systems. How do you reconcile these observations with the following two characteristics of most real-time programs: (a) the program never terminates or halts (if the system is functioning properly), and (b) a real-time program, at its highest level, is an endless loop.

2 Servicing an External Device

The enormous variety of microprocessor designs in currently operating real-time systems notwithstanding, there are but two basic strategies for the processor to communicate with the device: polling and interrupts. The choice of one strategy over the other has heavy implications for the design of any system.

In order to gain an intuitive notion of the distinction between polling and interrupts, let us suppose that the government (federal, state, and local taken as a whole) is the processor/controller in a real-time system and that your family is an external, controlled device. Now it is no coincidence that when the Bureau of the Census approaches you, that encounter is called a *poll*. You did not invite the poll-taker to come to your door, nor did you determine the frequency of the poll. (When the visit did finally occur, however, you were not caught by total surprise. You were expecting it, but you did not know when.) And although the Census is highly concerned about the number of people in your family, you do not contact the Bureau of the Census upon the event of a birth or death in the family. Those statistics (while they are called "vital") are not so critical to the statistical bookkeeping of the nation that they can't wait until the next whole decade before they are reported to the Bureau of Census. You wait for the Census to come to you for the information. The important point of the analogy is that while the government is responding to real events in your family (births and deaths, among other things), they are responding in such a way that the schedule of the government is in no way perturbed. Whole families may be (and sometimes are) wiped out by tragedy, but the Bureau of the Census does not "respond" to that change of state until it is time (government-type time) to do so. In order for the schedule of the Census to change (as might be necessary, for example, in the event of massive radiation disease affecting the whole nation), it would be necessary for Congress to change the design of the system. (If this last example has seemed too morbid, the reader is welcome to substitute the notion of the birth of sextuplets in every family; the point will be the same.)

For an analogy to discuss interrupts, we shall use government taxation on personal real estate. (Those readers living in states with no property tax must use their imaginations.) While the Bureau of the Census operates in a manner which we may call "not terribly responsive" to immediate changes in conditions, the assessment and collection of property taxes is "highly responsive" to any change in the status of a family's property, and the response is immediate. When a home is built, its value is recorded immediately in the assessor's office. When any major home improvement is done, the issuance of the mandatory building permit assures that the value of the improvement is also recorded for tax purposes. And whenever the property changes hands, the sale of the home will probably include an immediate sales tax payment plus a revised assessed valuation in the assessor's books. All the administrative overhead that state and county offices maintain is for the purpose of our "getting the immediate attention" of the tax office (whether we appreciate the attention or not). In the computer-control sense, we may say that we are "interrupting" whatever is going on in the assessor's office when the tax status of our home changes. And to stretch the analogy perhaps to the breaking point, we should note that the "routine" of the assessor's office is meant to be interrupted; interruptibility itself is their task of highest priority, as charged by the government. In a systems timing sense, though certainly not in the political sense, we can say that we as homeowners control the tax office, since it is totally our schedule of building, improving, buying and selling that prompts a change in our property valuation. (This ignores completely the factor of appreciation of the property even when changes are made and the home is not sold.)

To summarize, a controlling system polls an external device when and only so often as when the controlling system's original scheduling design tells it to. But a controlling system may be so designed with sufficient "overhead capability" that it may respond immediately to any pertinent events or changes of state in the external device; we say that such a system is *interrupt-driven*. (The term *event-driven* may be more accurate, since *interrupt* implies that something important must remain suspended while the device is serviced. We have already established that in a properly designed event-driven system, nothing is more important than servicing the device.)

Every decision in engineering design involves tradeoff considerations, and the decision to build a polled or event-driven system involves some fundamental issues.

1. Who is really to be in control? In an event-driven system, the device may seize control of the processor any time it "desires," leaving the nonforeground tasks suspended, perhaps for long periods of time (as processor time goes).

2. How is the code to be executed? In a polled system, the code is always executed sequentially, with all device service routines to commence at a known point in the program and to terminate and return to a known point. Interrupt service routines, as we shall see later, may occur between any two statements in the entire program.

3. Is the criticality of response time to the device worth the extra effort in design and debugging of interrupt-driven software? With proper care in the design and coding of an interrupt-driven program, the system integration and checkout phase of the system may be relatively free of anguish, but the nature of interrupt-driven routines is such that there is always a lurking uncertainty as to the origin of the "next bug." Interrupt-driven logic being what it is, that level of uncertainty is raised dramatically by the presence of certain routines that can demand execution at virtually any time.

4. But can the quality of responsiveness to the device stand the initial luxury (and relative ease) of a strictly polled system? If a processor has absolutely no other tasks than that of servicing the external device, then a very tight and very frequent poll of the status of the device would guarantee adequate "coverage" of the device. However, the typical system has the processor performing many levels of tasks, as previously noted (even though there may be only a single external device). In that sort of system, if the device cannot be polled frequently enough to guarantee adequate service, then polling is inadequate. Furthermore, in terms of modifying the system to incorporate more nonforeground tasks, a polled system may become unwieldy and inadequate, just because "that last necessary feature" had to be added. In the interest of system longevity, therefore, it is wiser (though perhaps more difficult at first) to design an interrupt-driven program from the start.

Let us now trace the flow of events during the actual execution of two different systems, one polling and the other interrupt-driven.

```
POLING:
    Statement 1: . . . .
    Statement 2: . . . .
    Statement 3: . . . .
    Statement 4: Do DSR
    Statement 5: . . . .
    Statement 6: Branch to Statement 1

DSR:        ;Device Service Routine
            Execute code to service device
            Return to interrupted routine
INTRPT:     ;DSR MAY INTERRUPT ANYWHERE
    Statement 1: . . . .
    Statement 2: . . . .
    Statement 3: . . . .
    Statement 4: . . . .
    Statement 5: . . . .
    Statement 6: Jump to Statement 1

DSR:        ;Interrupt-driven version
            Execute code to service device
            Return to wherever calling routine was interrupted
```

The most notable difference between these two sequences is that in POLING Statement 4 branches explicitly to DSR in order to service the external device just following Statement 3 and just before Statement 5—a branching and return operation whose sequence is just as predictable as the sequence of statements in the main program itself. In INTRPT, however, the device service routine gets executed whenever the device itself "wants" to be serviced. (We shall see later that the interrupting mechanism of the processor can be enabled and disabled at the discretion of the programmer; but in a typical system, the external device is allowed to interrupt at almost any time.) Of course the designer/programmer knows approximately how frequently in real time the device will interrupt for service, and the total elapsed time needed to execute the service routine will also be known, but neither the designer nor the main sequential code of INTRPT can "know" precisely where in the program the interrupt will occur. We only know that it will occur between any two statements in the program. The difference in our knowledge of the moment at which interrupts may occur appears rather trivial in a program whose sequential code comprises only six statements. However, in a program with perhaps thousands of statements, the real power of interrupt service routines becomes immediately apparent. We can always be certain that the external device will get the processor when it needs it (within the time it takes for the currently executing instruction to be completed and for the processor to "remember" where it was executing at the time of the interrupt—all this in just a few microseconds). Furthermore, as designers of the total system, we feel free to "ignore" the needs of the device once the interrupt service routines have been written. We are free to write whatever code we feel is necessary for the nonforeground activity of the system, knowing that the interrupting mechanism of the processor will assure adequate attention to the device.

But there are some precautions the designer must observe in a system that add significant background activity to the foreground work of servicing external devices. The most apparent danger (and the one we can discuss now) is that the foreground activity of the processor may be so frequent, or the interrupt routine(s) may be so lengthy, that the background activity may be squeezed out, never getting executed at all, or very little. The is only one of many instances in which the software specialist must be highly aware of the specifications of the device to be serviced by the processor: How fast does it accomplish the task it was designed for? How frequently will it demand servicing by the processor in the worst (i.e., most frequent) case? Is the hardware interface to the microcomputer designed in a highly general manner, such that the software must expend considerable time assigning a precise meaning to an interrupt, for example? We shall be looking at such problems in close detail later when we design a system for data communication.

Polling and Interrupts: Implementation

We have thus far pointed out only the general considerations relative to device interfaces. In this section I shall deal specifically with how to implement in 8080 assembler the two major strategies for communicating with a peripheral device: polling (flag-checking) and interrupts.

Polling

For the example application, let us design an initial version of an atmospheric-sensitive carburetor system. In a fully automated and fully optimized system, the device would respond to differences in temperature, humidity, air density, and perhaps other factors. For our example, we shall concentrate only on the parameter of temperature. As might be expected, the necessary interface data structure (control/status register, or CSR) is as terse as could be found; it consists of but two meaningful bits, which we shall define as follows:

Bit number	Function	Interpretations
0	Status	0: Intake air below normal operating temperature
		1: Intake air at or above normal operating temperature
1	Control	0: Allow minimum air intake (rich fuel mix)
		1: Allow maximum air intake (lean fuel mix)

(Note that this version of the product is even more crude than we described earlier, inasmuch as both the status and control functions are all or nothing. Such a system would, of course, be unacceptable in a finished product.)

The algorithm for implementing this "solid-state choking" system is very straightforward, as in any algorithm that incorporates polling as the means of device interfacing.

1. *Initiate the system by calling for minimum air intake (rich fuel).*

In terms of the CSR, we wish to turn off (set to zero) bit number 1. (Since future versions of the device most likely will make use of the other bits in the CSR, we must be careful to turn off *only* bit 1 and to leave the other bits unchanged.) The code necessary to accomplish this is indeed brief:

```
;
; ROUTINE TO SET CARBURETOR FOR MINIMUM AIR INTAKE
;
; MEANING OF VARIABLES:
;        CRBPRT ("CARBURETOR PORT"): I/O PORT
;                FOR ACCESS TO AND FROM CSR
;        AIRMIX: BIT PATTERN WITH ONLY BIT 1 CLEAR
;                (11111101) [BINARY]
```

```
IN      CRBPRT  ;"COPY" THE CSR INTO THE
                ;    ACCUMULATOR
ANI     AIRMIX  ;MAKE BIT 1 = 0, LEAVING
                ;    ALL OTHER BITS ALONE
OUT     CRBPRT  ;MOVE THAT (POSSIBLY) REVISED
                ;    CSR WORD BACK TO "REAL"
                ;    CSR LOCATION
```

(For the moment, we shall not concern ourselves with how the actual 8080 instructions accomplish what the comments say. All this will be covered in a later chapter on the instruction set.)

In the preceding sequence, the actual bit configuration could have been specified in binary, as follows:

```
ANI 11111101B
```

Note the ease in accomplishing I/O; the two commands IN and OUT move a word into and out of the accumulator, respectively. The programmer previously assigns the I/O port a symbolic name, if he desires that a name be used, as in the example. Such a name assignment might be accomplished by the following statement, located probably in some initialization routine in the code:

```
CRBPRT EQU    n    ; n IS THE
                   ;  NUMBER OF THE I/O PORT
```

If certain interface devices are used with the 8080, then the ports are referenced even more simply, by a digit. The entire issue of defining ports for I/O is totally a function of the hardware selected for the system and the decisions made between hardware and software designers in the implementation of a particular system. Therefore we shall say here only that the programmer needs to remember the two assembler commands IN and OUT, plus the port numbering or memory location assignment conventions agreed upon among the designers for the particular hardware configuration.

2. *Execute a polling loop.*

As stated earlier, non-real-time programmers fear loops, particularly loops in which there is no internal mechanism to allow for an orderly escape. But this is the essence of event-driven software; the only mechanism for getting free of the loop in nearly every instance must originate in the outside world.

Before we dive into actual code for the polling loop, let us state in clear English what the loop is really to accomplish:

1. Examine the CSR of the device controller.
2. See whether bit 0 is set (= 1) or clear (= 0). In checking bit 0, we are monitoring the intake air temperature: 0 = cold, 1 = normal.
3. If bit 0 is set, then clear bit 1; if bit 0 is clear, then set bit 1. Bit 1 controls the amount of air to the carburetor.
4. Write the revised CSR to the output port of the device.

Next, we must modify the English somewhat so that our (hopefully) unambiguous English resembles formal computer code:

```
1   GET CSR CONTENTS INTO ACCUMULATOR
2   SAVE CONTENTS OF CSR
3   ISOLATE BIT 0 IN ACCUMULATOR
4   IF BIT 0 IS SET
5   THEN
6      CLEAR BIT 1 IN CSR
7   ELSE
8      SET BIT 1 IN CSR
9   END
10  PUT ACCUMULATOR CONTENTS INTO CSR
11  RETURN TO CALLING ROUTINE
```

Note that END is simply a syntactic device to define the limit of the IF . . . THEN . . . ELSE block. Actual run-time execution of the block would proceed in one of two ways: 4-5-6-9-10 or 4-7-8-9-10.

Now study the following sequence, without being concerned for the moment as to what each assembler statement means. The number in the comment field corresponds generally to the line numbers of the preceding "pseudo-code."

```
; DEVICE SERVICE LOOP TO ADJUST CARBURETOR AIR
; ACCORDING TO INTAKE AIR TEMPERATURE
;
TMPADJ:  IN      CRBCSR   ; (1)
         PUSH    PSW      ; (2)
         ANI     01H      ; (3)
         JNZ     THEN01   ; (4)
         JZ      ELSE01   ;
THEN01:  POP     PSW      ; (5)
         ANI     0FDH     ; (6)
         JMP     END01    ;
ELSE01:  POP     PSW      ; (7)
         ORI     02H      ; (8)
END01:   OUT     CRBCSR   ; (10)
         RET              ; (11)
```

The reader will note (1) that there is not a one-for-one correspondence between pseudo-code statements and assembly language instructions and (2) that instruction 4 is logically inverted between the two versions. However, we should emphasize that except for these minor discrepancies, we have observed a remarkably smooth transition from English narrative to actual assembler code. We shall examine this procedure in some depth in a separate chapter.

One line of the preceding code that will probably be totally baffling to the reader is the ANI 0FDH instruction. Briefly, FD are hexadecimal digits that comprise an 8-bit byte in which only bit 1 is low; the H informs the compiler of the code that FD are hexadecimal digits.

Interrupts

In the case of polling, we gained the impression that the sequential code was always well in control of things. The actual sequence of instructions determined precisely in what order each task was to be accomplished, including the task of polling the external device. This sort of strategy implied that the status bits (only a single bit in our crude example) are of critical importance in controlling the device. The program determines when it will poll the device, and it is up to the program to interrogate the device. This interrogation consists of reading the status bit(s) of the CSR of the device; hence the term *flag-checking*, which is often used when referring to a polling strategy. Once again, note that the device is a rather passive creature in this scheme, while the sequential code being executed by the processor is very domineering, very much in control of the schedule of events.

With an interrupt-driven system, we basically concede some scheduling authority to the external device, at the expense of the tidy, unperturbed, totally sequential world of the central processor. No longer does the device sit idly by, passively awaiting interrogation by the processor. Now the device itself is empowered essentially to say "I need servicing now" whenever it pleases and to get the service almost whenever it pleases.

Our task in this section will be to see precisely how we enable the device to get the processor's attention, as we so dramatized it previously. (The reader who is bothered by this discussion, which treats hardware in almost a human manner, attributing an independent will and even desires to the external device, should withhold judgment until seeing the terminology used even in very technical discussions.)

As we consider the actual coding implementation of interrupt-handling, the most important difference is that with interrupts we do not "call the device in," as we seemed to do with the IN CSR instruction in the preceding polling routine. Rather, the device simply "comes in" when it "wants to," regardless of what the microprocessor may be doing at that particular moment. For the programmer with a distaste for untidiness, the prospect of an interrupt-driven system may sound hideously messy and unpredictable. And indeed, we must admit at the outset that debugging external-event-driven software can be extremely difficult for the obvious reason that we can never be certain whether a bug is occurring within the sequential code or within the interrupt-servicing code, or whether the device's unannounced intrusion within the sequential code has itself caused some problem in the software suddenly to come to the surface.

Having admitted to the inherent problems of interrupt-driven code, we now must consider the very clean and orderly manner in which a particular processor (the 8080 and 8085) has been designed to facilitate interrupt software. Bear in mind that the design philosophy we are about to study and to apply is the only one of a half dozen or more strategies now found among the various microprocessors. The order of events in the total interrupt process are as follows:

1. The programmer enables the interrupt mechanism of the microprocessor from within the code itself. This is accomplished by the single instruction EI (enable interrupts). Until interrupts are enabled, there is nothing that any external device can do to stop the internal sequential flow of instructions in the processor.

2. The device itself, when it decides that it needs to be serviced (i.e., when it is time to execute the particular block of code necessary to perform the service needed by the device), requests an interrupt from the processor.

3. The processor acknowledges the request from the interrupting device.

4. The processor completes the instruction it is currently executing.

5. The processor automatically disables any further interrupts from any device.

6. The processor stores on the stack (at the location pointed to by SP, the stack pointer) the memory address of the next instruction to be executed, once the interrupting device has been serviced.

7. The interrupting device (the one already acknowledged) directs the processor to a prearranged location in low memory (a vector). Another way of saying this is that the program counter is loaded with a memory location associated with the device. We shall discuss shortly some alternative methods for achieving this apparently magical process.

8. With the program counter now loaded with the address of a particular low-memory location (vector), the processor begins to execute the instructions located at that particular location. An interrupting device will typically require more service than can be rendered by instructions that will fit into the 8 bytes allowed for in the low-memory vector. Consequently, the programmer of interrupt service routines for the 8080/8085 will normally place a CALL to the "real" service routine, one which can occupy as much memory as is necessary. That CALL is followed by an EI and a RET; we shall explain presently what these two instructions accomplish.

9. The "real" service routine is executed. This constitutes the code needed to "service" the external device in the manner described by the requirements of the system. In the case of the carburetor previously described, when the heat reaches a certain threshold, as agreed upon by the designers, the CSR bit controlling the air intake is toggled.

10. Upon reaching the RET instruction in the "real" service routine, control passes back to the "short" routine in the low-memory vector area, where the next instruction is an EI. This will re-enable interrupts to the processor after one further instruction has been executed. (The entire interrupting mechanism of the processor has been disabled during all these steps in servicing the device whose interrupt was first acknowledged.)

11. The RET instruction causes the program counter now to be loaded with the address of the "main" code that was originally interrupted by the device's request. That address (2 bytes) is "popped" back into the program counter from the stack.

12. With the program counter now restored, the "main" sequential code of the program continues on as it was at the time of the interrupt.

Although the blow-by-blow of how an interrupt is processed may seem a bit obscure, the operations are actually rather straightforward. The exception to this is the method for generating the RST (RESTART) instruction, the instruction that "drives" the processor to a precise vector location in low memory. There is actually a variety of ways for this instruction to be generated. In the 8080 processor, one way for this to happen is for the device to generate the instruction RST n, where n is a number from 0 to 7. That particular instruction comprises only a single byte, and is laid out as follows: $111xxx11$. The xxx bits may assume a value between 0 and 7, a value that in turn directs execution to a unique 8-byte segment of code loaded ahead of time in low memory.

There are several design options for enabling the device to generate an RST instruction. One is for the 8 bits to be generated entirely by designer-built hardware logic, a common and simple procedure for systems comprising a single interrupting device. A programmable peripheral interface may also be used, particularly where multiple devices are to be handled. If a PPI is used, then a wide variety of techniques may be employed in the interrupt system. The actual operation of such a product is beyond the scope of this discussion and should be studied in detail in the respective manuals.

In the case of the 8085, the designer's task is even simpler. The interrupting device need only be tied (i.e., connected) to the processor such that the interrupting pulse enters through one of the three pins on the processor chip itself. In this way, when the device pulses the processor for an interrupt, the processor itself generates the proper RST instruction. Depending on the pin connected to the interrupting device, execution of the interrupt-mode program would commence at location 2CH, 34H, or 3CH (8 bytes of instruction space per interrupt pin selected).

The reader should be surprised to learn that it takes but eight software instructions to implement all the preceding logic. The reason for this is that when a device in this system interrupts and requests service, there is no need for any decision-making logic to determine its status. The service routine can simply assume that it needs to be serviced. Thus there is nothing like an IF . . . THEN . . . ELSE needed, as in the polling routine.

Although the code is brief and simple, it is spread over the system in four distinct locations. We shall trace execution of the interrupt servicing through these four locations: initialization, device, vector, main memory.

1. *Initialization.* In order for the processor's interrupt mechanism to function properly, the programmer must first enable interrupts. This is accomplished (normally within an initialization routine that is executed only once) by the simple instruction EI   ;ENABLE INTERRUPTS. Recall that the interrupt mechanism has (within the hardware itself) the ability to acknowledge an interrupt request, disable further interrupts, store the program counter on the stack, and store the processor status flags on the stack.

2. *Device.* By one of the means previously suggested, the external device must assume responsibility to issue a RST (RESTART) instruction. (In the 8085, the processor itself can generate the instruction.) That instruction will assume the form

```
RST n     ;n IS THE SEQUENCE NUMBER
          ;  OF THE VECTOR SPACE CON-
          ;  TAINING THE CODE SHOWN
          ;  BELOW
```

The *n* argument of the RST instruction is actually a multiple of 8 (hexadecimal), which specifies which 8-byte block of low memory the processor is now directed to. Thus, a RST 1 will cause the program to branch to location 0008, RST 2 will cause a branch to 10 (hexadecimal), RST 3 will send it to 18, and so on.

3. *Vector.* Normally three instructions would be inserted at the vector location (0008H, 0010H, 0018H, or whatever address) specified by the RST instruction. The instructions would be

```
ORG     0008H     ; INTERRUPT CODE STARTS HERE
CALL    ISR001    ; (1)
EI                ; (2)
RET               ; (3)
```

This sequence has the effect of (1) calling the user-written device service routine, (2) re-enabling interrupts to the processor, once the service routine has been executed, and (3) returning to whatever the processor was doing when the interrupt occurred.

4. *Main memory*. The device service routine itself will look like any other subroutine. In the case of this application, the routine will appear simpler than the polling routine because it is strictly sequential with no decision branches. The four instructions comprising this routine are

```
ISR001:                    ;
        IN      2          ;(1)
        ORI     02H        ;(2)
        OUT     2          ;(3)
        RET                ;(4)
```

These four instructions accomplish the following functions. First, the contents of the CSR are moved into the accumulator from I/O port number 2. (The notions of I/O port and interrupt location should not be confused.) Second, we do not need to interrogate the status of the device this time. Since an interrupt has occurred from this device, we know (by the design of the system) that now is the time to set bit 1 of the CSR. This instruction sets that bit in the "copy" of the CSR now residing in the accumulator. Third, that updated copy of the CSR, whose bit 1 is now set, is moved back into the actual CSR. It is at this moment that actual control of the device occurs. Fourth, (RETURN) this causes the processor to return to the instruction immediately following the CALL, which is in this case would be the EI in the vector area specified by the RST command from the device.

Naturally, in a real-life system the "main memory" interrupt service routine would be longer than four instructions. If such a routine were really that brief, then it should be executed within the vector space itself (the 08H area), without an additional CALL.

The entire interrupt-driven system represents an interesting orchestration of effort shared by the hardware designer, the software programmer, and the processor itself. The responsibilities of each "participant" may be listed as follows:

1. *The hardware designer* enables device to issue the RST *n* instruction to processor. With the 8085, the hardware designer ties the external device to one of three interrupt pins on the microprocessor chip.
2. *The software designer/programmer* places appropriate CALL, EI, and RET instructions at the low-memory location corresponding to *n* in RST instruction and writes interrupt service routine.
3. *The processor*, when interrupted, "remembers" location of next instruction to be executed following RET from vector location and disables interrupts when RST is executed.

Now that we have implemented a realistic piece of logic using both polling (flag-checking) and interrupts, the reader no doubt feels that much verbiage has been expended for very few lines of actual code. Such an observation constitutes perhaps the most salient characteristic of real-time programming: the very few lines of code reflect profound design decisions and may often hide a high degree of complexity.

Exercises

2-1. One shorthand way of describing the difference between a system that uses polling and one that uses interrupts is to say that in the former the computer is in control of the device while in the latter the external device is in control of the computer. Enlarge upon this, using a somewhat more concise description.

2-2. Programmers frequently distinguish between "logic bugs" and "real-time bugs" in a system, the real-time variety being the most dreaded. Elaborate upon this distinction, and tell why the latter type of bug is usually the worst.

2-3. The 12 components of the protocol necessary for servicing interrupts may be divided between tasks that are performed by the programmer in code and those which are accomplished purely by hardware at run-time. a. Identify which activities from the list are done by the applications software written by the programmer. Describe briefly the problem(s) that would result should each of these activities fail (one at a time). Give a single description for each type of failure. b. Do the same for the purely hardware tasks.

2-4. That same list of 12 protocol components may be used in the case of debugging or trouble-shooting a system in which interrupt service routines do not seem to be executing properly. Use the list of protocol steps to construct a checklist of questions that may be used in diagnosing the system.

3 Interfacing with an External Device

Rather than attempt even an informal definition of a device interface, we shall approach this topic rather obliquely by means of a fable. The discriminating reader who either (1) dislikes fiction in any form or (2) appreciates only good fiction should skip immediately to the end of the fable. All others (and the author sincerely hopes that there will be some) should keep alert to the meaning of the fable for real-time computing.

Where Communication Happens: The Control/Status Register

The Liberator of Megamuralia: A Fable

Long ago, in the year 1238 to be exact, in the Kingdom of Microterrania there ruled a king named Pachycephalius II, PC II for short. Now while it is common knowledge that historians attribute the king's eccentric behavior to a certain deficiency of wit (all the citizens of Microterrania were at least second cousins), there are several reputable writers who ascribe to the king what some analysts today would call simply a "fixation." It is said that every ruler views his *noblesse oblige* to be that of leaving his mark on the world; and in the case of Pachycephalius, the mark was unmistakable and in fact manifested rather early in his reign. While some kings are remembered for their many wives, for the size of their wardrobe, for their private real estate, or for their ability in the fine arts, King PC II was noted for what Professor Schmidt calls a "wall fixation." Whether it was because he remained unattended for too long a time in his spacious nursery while an infant isn't certain, but we do know that he subsequently developed an insatiable craving for walls. Chess, tennis, and polo, the customary pastimes of the aristocracy and landed gentry gave way to handball, hang gliding (from atop high walls), and squash (it just seemed more patriotic). In the arts, sculpting and oil painting all but ceased in favor of weaving massive tapestries and producing frescoes. Walls even became the king's universal solution to the political ills of the realm. Whenever feuding erupted between disputing heirs apparent to the throne, the king would simply command walls to be erected between the parties involved—far more humane than the fratricidal bloodbaths customary to that time. But most notable was the very architecture of Megamuralia, the capital city (which comprised 81.37 percent of the total kingdom). Every visitor to the city agreed that the Megamuralian walls were like none other: thick, high, and well-defended. The king even offered a 25 percent housing subsidy to anyone who would build his home against the inside of the city wall, thereby making the city wall that much thicker.

The only problem with all this was that the king had, so to speak, put all his raisins in one cupcake. For while Megamuralia's walls were its pride, the gates were its shame. The technology of hinges had not reached Microterrania as yet, and the Ministry of Security had to settle for the best their contractors could provide: large planks lashed together with rawhide laces and attached to the walls with fragments of adhesive goat bladders. In addition, the discrepancy in personnel was even more deplorable. Whereas the walls were patrolled by dozens of well-drilled platoons of deadly archers, the royal budget could support only two small (albeit loyal) security squads to guard all 15 of the city gates. (The Minister of Finance had not yet learned of deficit spending.) Since it was impossible for the men to cover all the gates all the time, their entire defense strategy was based on the principle of "random concentration." The two squads would move about the city, spending varying periods of time at the different gates. Any attacker was thereby assured that he *might* clash head-on with half the entire gate security force (seven retired accountants) if he were to attack through a city gate.

By and by the people of Microterrania became concerned that there might be things more exciting than housing subsidies and handball, so they secretly conspired with the king's eldest son Al-khuwarizmus[a] for the overthrow of the government. Since nearly every available male in the kingdom was employed either in defending the wall or the city gates of Megamuralia, big Al (as he was affectionately known to his coconspirators) knew straightway that this was a job for mercenaries.

For all his deficiencies, the king was not blind to political unrest. To prevent a possible overthrow, he had Big Al locked in his bedchamber each night, and left him with only his nightgown, toothbrush, and eight aromatic votive candlesticks (for use in his private worship and devotional reading). As the king always said, "Al may indeed be a treacherous cutthroat, but he is basically a fine lad."

And so every day Al roamed the city and near environs of Megamuralia, and every night he retired in a state of house arrest to his bedchamber, there to burn his candles and look out from the city wall. One night the city was suddenly overrun by 18 Bedouin mercenaries, and the people cried, "Long live Al-khuwarizmus I." The erstwhile king asked respectfully, "How did you do it, my son? The terrain without the gates is impossible to traverse for all but natives like ourselves, and none of these foreigners were ever seen in the realm before. How did they ever find their way through the rugged underbrush to that unguarded gate?"

---

[a]Named after the Arab mathematician of the same name, from which the word *algorithm* is derived. The son was so named while being held for ransom in a North African slave camp, having been kidnapped by Byzantine marauders.

"Elementary, my dear father," replied his son. "I met with these mercenaries yesterday afternoon, after they had watered their camels two furlongs thither, and we devised the plan within 30 minutes." "Say on," said his father dully, "for the strategy eludes me yet."

"Recall that there are but two windows in my chamber, one that affords full view of the gates of the Fiery Locust, the Green Carob Nut, and the Giant Jackal. The other window, the one looking out through the city wall, was fortified a fortnight ago (at your command) by the royal masons so that now it is in effect eight little windows in one. [There were now eight small, open "panes" where there had been a single opening; the concept of panes was also unknown in Microterrania. Hence Al's groping for words.] To each of these tiny windows, each the height of a single candle, the soldiers and I agreed to the following code." He explained how each sector of the window should be numbered, as in Figure 3-1. And the meanings attributed to each candle, according to its placement, should be as follows:

Candle	Meaning
1	Candle on: signal is complete; go ahead and read it now
	Candle off: wait for me to complete the signal

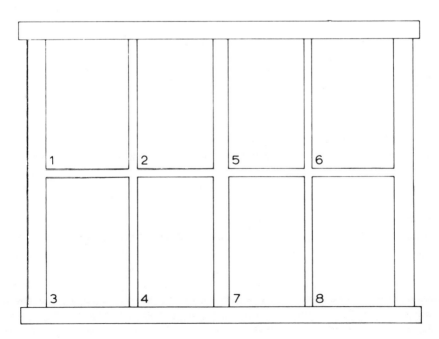

Figure 3-1. "Window Code" Assignments in Fable.

Candle	Meaning
2, 3, 4	Seven possible commands, depending on the particular candles on and off: 001, 010, 011, 100, 101, 110, 111
	001: Move soldiers toward the gate whose number is indicated by candles 5 through 8
	010: Head for cover! Mounted patrols searching area outside walls.
	011: Advance toward the wall the number of furlongs indicated by candles 5 through 8
	100: Move left the number furlongs indicated
	101: Move right the number of furlongs indicated
	110: Verify to me the number passed in the previous message (that was an important one, and I want to be doubly sure you got it right)
	111: Attack now (through the gate whose number is indicated)
5–8	A number 0 through 15, specified by the particular candles lighted

Likewise, the soldiers' fires were assigned meanings as follows:

Fires visible to Al	Meaning
1	We don't see the message clearly yet; leave it on.
2	We copy
3	(When applicable) We're done with that command. Send the next one
4	We're dousing the fires for awhile; suspect enemy nearby
Any permutation	A single number from 0 to 15, used to verify numbers

The historical records are sparse concerning the reign of Al-khuwarizmus I, but there is some reason to believe that the king and his Minister of Finance, who happened to be entranced with hexadecimal numbers, formed a private company for the training of promising young government workers, called Incipient Bureaucrats of Microterrania. Some of the students became proficient in hexadecimal calculations, using vast banks of candles, 16 candles to a rack, 1000 racks to a bank. But since the initials of the company were neither pronounceable as a single word nor were derived from any known deity, the company itself slipped gradually into disrepute and finally into smug decadence.

The reader has no doubt found it obvious that the window in the wall was a device interface mechanism between the king's son (central processor) and the outside world. The campfires, on the other hand, served as the interface between the mercenaries (external device) and the world that was external to them. The window and the campfires taken together therefore constitute an entire and sufficient means of communication (both ways) between the "central processor" and the "external device." In the remainder of this chapter, we shall generalize from some of the observations regarding interface problems as seen through the fable. We shall first propose two working definitions and then list some important observations.

1. *Communication:* transmission of data between two or more independently functioning subsystems such that the state of the system as a whole is altered in a meaningful manner.

2. *Communications protocol:* the set of rules that is essential to proper transmission of data between communications subsystems and has been mastered by each subsystem prior to actual data transmission.

Finally, we wish to make some observations of interface strategies in general.

1. The interface data structure is typically very concise, containing no redundant information.

2. The conventions established in the design of the system protocol dictate the semantics of the interface structure components. Each bit position in the structure must convey a truth value relating to a predetermined condition (e.g., the device is busy/not busy; error A did/did not occur.

3. There is normally no direct physical relation between the interface data structure and the actual events or states the structure represents. The assignment of the positions of the various bits in a control/status structure is arbitrary and follows the design convention established by the designer of the system.

4. In all communications systems there is a certain amount of overhead necessary just to assure the integrity of the transmitted data. This is actually a paraphrase of the definition of protocol. In the fable, window pane 1 and command 6 were protocol-related items, as were fires 1 through 3 of the soldiers.

5. Communication in the oral (and, to some extent, written) mode normally serves to overcome discontinuities in space. In a computer system, one strives mainly to overcome discontinuities in time (i.e., by getting one independently functioning subsystem "synced" with another), and the issue of spatial separation between subsystems is practically an afterthought. If the systems are separate at all, then the thickness of the wall or the distance between the components makes no difference.

6. In a microcomputer system, the microprocessor is typically viewed as the "intelligent" host or "master," while the device being controlled is a "slave" having considerably less intelligence than the microprocessor.

7. There is a degree of "blindness" assumed on the part of both the master and slave. (The cover of night and the random movements of the security forces guaranteed a high degree of ignorance on the part of the invading forces. It is a wise design philosophy to assume no mutual knowledge between the host and slave, and then to specify the minimum information necessary for the proper functioning of the system.

8. Viewed from the standpoint of the computer, the typical interface data structure has the functions of (1) reporting status and (2) exerting control. Hence the name *control/status register* (CSR) which is normally applied to such a structure.

36

Exercises

3-1. In the design of a CSR, it is necessary to specify which of the bits are *read-only* (unable to be written to by the software) and which are *writable* by the program software. Consider the CSR of a typical card reader. The following functions (among others) would be represented in the register: (a) device off-line (turned off); (b) data error (too many holes in column of card); (c) ready; (d) read (command); and (e) interrupt enable. Which of these would probably be read-only bits? For each bit, tell why the bit would probably be read-only or read-write. (Note: hardware designers may opt for certain bits or even whole memory areas to be write-only.)

3-2. In the case of a device with several possible error conditions to report through the CSR, it would be cumbersome for the program to query each bit in order to determine whether an error has occurred. What hardware design strategy might assist programming at this point?

3-3. In most real-time applications in which the transfer of data is part of the system, those data are normally sent and received through data buffers assigned to the device rather than through the CSR of the device. In the fable, the "device CSR" (the prince's window panes) comprised both CSR and data buffer functions, "data" in this case being simply numbers and not control functions. Identify the "output data buffer" (for data sent by the prince) and the "input data buffer" (for data transmitted by the mercenaries). For each case, tell what determines that the particular data bits are to be treated as data bits rather than as control/status bits.

3-4. How can the phrase "the controlled device is the slave" be reconciled with the comment in Chapter 2 that in a polling strategy "the device is in control."

3-5. Would it be a feasible design strategy to connect a device CSR and device data buffer directly to a remote line connecting the host processor with the external device. (Recall that in a remote communications system the data are nearly always transmitted a single bit at a time.

4

Representing Data (How They Look)

No matter what the word length of a particular computer might be, and no matter which numbering system is used, the storage and manipulation of data in a digital computer are realized ultimately as individual bits. Theoretically, it would be perfectly acceptable to reduce all code and data to binary (base 2) form at the outset when working with a computer—acceptable to the computer, that is, and an outrageous imposition to the programmer/user. For the sake of readability and transportability, therefore, the binary code and data are represented for the 8080 (as for most modern computers) in hexadecimal (base 16) notation when the bits are considered in groups of four, in octal (base 8) for bit groupings of 3, and in binary when the user wishes to remain in control of individual bits (as in the case of a bit mask used in a compare operation). In this brief chapter we shall survey the various environments of numeric code and data in the software of a typical user. Then we shall describe how the various number formats (decimal, hexadecimal, octal, and binary) are specified to the 8080 assembler.

Code as Numbers

Although the programmer normally considers his instructions in terms of mnemonic op codes (such as MOV for a move instruction or LDA for loading something into the accumulator), the computer will ultimately execute those instructions after they have been changed to binary form (i.e., compiled). For example, the following instruction says that a value of 3 is being moved to the accumulator:

MVI   A,03

The compiled (binary) form of the instruction would occupy two 8-bit bytes in the 8080 and would be encoded into binary form (compiled) as follows:

0011 1110   The "move" portion of the instruction
0000 0011   The data portion of the instruction (= 3)

Those groups of four bits within each byte of the instruction and data in this example would appear thus (in hexadecimal form):

```
3E 03        ;MOVE 3 INTO THE ACCUMULATOR
```

We are making a special point of the numeric representation of code since a listing of a compiled program will normally show this numeric form for the code in the second column of the listing, as shall be pointed out below. And even with very elaborate software development systems, the programmers frequently must work with the instructions in numeric form during on-line debugging. After some length of time, a programmer becomes very accustomed to code as numbers. Note the hexadecimal representation of the program in Figure 4-1. The numeric code is printed toward the left in the listing.

Data as Numbers

Numbers are most often associated with data in the common sense rather than with code. Let us now look at user-supplied data in the context of (1) immediate-mode instructions and (2) value initialization of data space in memory.

Data may be included as part of an instruction. After the program is compiled, those data are carried along immediately following the "move" command portion of the instruction; hence the term *immediate mode*. Study the program listing in Figure 4-1. Note how the immediate data in the source code become part of the compiled "object" code. Or consider the following instruction:

```
CPI     07     ;COMPARE CONTENTS OF
               ; ACCUMULATOR WITH 7
```

As a general rule of programming practice, it is preferable to use symbols or labels rather than immediate-mode data within the code itself. In this way, the single change made to a symbol or piece of data (in a separate symbol assignment or data section) will propagate itself automatically to wherever that symbol or labeled value is used.

Symbols as Numbers

Symbols can have their values set in two different ways on the 8080, one modifiable and the other permanent. The assembler directives are SET and EQU and are used as follows:

```
SYMBL1   SET     05     ;SYMBL1 = 5 AT FIRST
SYMBL1   SET     03     ; THEN = 3 LATER
SYMBL2   EQU     07     ;SYMBL2 = 07 THROUGHOUT
                        ; ENTIRE PROGRAM
```

```
LOC  OBJ     SEQ         SOURCE STATEMENT

              1  ; AUTHOR:      RON TURNER
              2  ; DATE 23-APR-78
              3  ; PURPOSE OF PROGRAM:
              4  ;     TO DEMONSTRATE RELATIONSHIP BETWEEN SYMBOLIC SOURCE CODE (AS WRITTEN
              5  ; BY THE PROGRAMMER) AND THE HEXADECIMAL CODE GENERATED BY THE ASSEMBLER
              6  ;
              7  ; NOTE THE THREE COLUMNS OF DATA GENERATED BY THE COMPILER (ASSEMBLER):
              8  ;     1. MEMORY LOCATION OF THE STATEMENT       "LOC"
              9  ;     2. HEXADECIMAL OBJECT CODE                "OBJ"
             10  ;     3. SOURCE CODE SEQUENCE NUMBER            "SEQ"
             11  ; IT IS THE HEXADECIMAL CODE THAT IS ACTUALLY EXECUTED BY THE COMPUTER AT RUN-TIME.
             12  ;
0000         13         ORG    00H       ;TELL COMPILER TO LOCATE CODE AT MEMORY ADDRESS ZERO
             14  TEST:
0000 06FE    15         MVI    B,0FEH    ;MOVE HEX FE INTO REGISTER B
0002 3EFF    16         MVI    A,0FFH    ;MOVE HEX FF INTO ACCUMULATOR
0004 DE0F    17         SBI    15        ;SUBTRACT DECIMAL 15 FROM CONTENTS OF ACCUMULATOR
0006 90      18         SUB    B         ;SUBTRACT CONTENTS OF B FROM ACCUMULATOR
             19  END                      ;TELL COMPILER THAT THIS IS THE PROGRAM'S END

PUBLIC SYMBOLS

EXTERNAL SYMBOLS

USER SYMBOLS
TEST    A 0000

ASSEMBLY COMPLETE, NO ERRORS
```

Figure 4-1. Example Program: Source versus Object Code.

Very frequently the programmer wishes to initialize some location in memory to a given value. The 8080 assembler directives DB and DW will accomplish this for bytes (8-bit units) and for words (16-bit units) of memory as in the following examples:

```
BYTES:    DB      123456    ;PLACES SIX ACTUAL BYTE-
                            ; LENGTH VALUES IN SUCCESSIVE
                            ; MEMORY LOCATIONS
WORDS:    DW      123456    ; PLACES SIX WORD-
                            ; LENGTH VALUES
```

The preceding labels are arbitrary names, selected by the programmer. The location of BYTES in memory is the starting point for the six successive byte values just defined. Likewise, the labeled location for WORDS is the start of the six successive word-length values initialized in the code. The use of the assembler directives SET, EQU, DB, and DW will be covered in further detail in Chapter 6.

Specification of Radix (Number Base)

These examples demonstrate the instances in which the user must supply actual numbers within the code: as part of immediate-mode instructions and within data definitions. Fortunately, the 8080 assembler was designed with the user in mind, such that great flexibility is allowed in specifying number format. If the coder simply writes a proper decimal number, with no identifying base indicator (as the 123456 above), then the compiler automatically (by default) assumes the number to be decimal. When the user wishes to use a hexadecimal number, he or she merely appends H to the number (0FEH, for example, for the hexadecimal number FE). For octal, the user appends the letter Q. There is already enough confusion between 0 (zero) and the letter O, so Q is definitely the preferred option. And for binary, the letter B is used (0011B would represent 3).

It would be excellent practice for the reader to scan any of the 8080 assembled listings in Chapter 13, paying particular attention to the second column, which contains the actual (hexadecimal) numeric representation of all the data used in the program.

Exercises

4-1. Write the binary and decimal equivalents of each of the following hexadecimal numbers: (a) 0BAH, (b) 0FEH, (c) 00DH, (d) 0A3H, (e) 020H.

4-2. Write the binary and hexadecimal equivalents for each of the following decimal numbers: (a) 205, (b) 131, (c) 100, (d) 199, (e) 064.

4-3. In this exercise the reader is asked to function as a compiler, i.e., to translate mnemonic op codes plus register/memory options into hexadecimal form. It would be helpful to do each instruction in binary first, and then to convert the result to hexadecimal. For the instructions in this question, assume the numeric code for the single registers to be as follows:

B: 0
C: 1
D: 2
E: 3
H: 4
L: 5
A: 7

For each different instruction, the instruction bits (given for that instruction) and the register option bits (depending on the register selected) are as follows:

DCR   *reg*   (Decrement the register indicated)
Bit assignments: 00*rrr*101
DCR   L compiled as: 0010 1101B and as 02DH

a. DCR   A

b. ANA   *reg*   (Logical AND with accumulator)
     Bit assignments: 10100*rrr*
     ANA   L
     ANA   A

c. ORA   *reg*   (OR *reg* with accumulator)
     Bit assignments: 10110rrr
     ORA   C
     ORA   D

d. XRA   *reg*   (EXCLUSIVE-OR *reg* with accumulator)
     Bit assignments: 10101*rrr*
     XRA   C
     XRA   B

e. INR   *reg*   (Increment *reg* specified)
    Bit assignments: 00*rrr*100
    INR   A
    INR   L

4-4. In instructions manipulating register pairs, the codes for the pairs are as follows:

B,C: 0
D,E: 1
H,L   2
SP   3

Now compile (first into binary, then into hexadecimal) the following instructions. Bit assignments are provided as in the previous question.

a. DCX   *rp*   (Decrement register pair)
    Bit assignments: 00*rr*1011
    DCX   H
    DCX   D
    DCX   SP

b. LDAX   *rp*   (Load accumulator with byte addressed by B, C or D,E
    Bit assignments: 000*r*1010
    LDAX   B
    LDAX   D

c. POP   *rp*   (Pop-top 2 bytes from stack to rp)
    Bit assignments: 11*rr*0001
    POP   D
    POP   H

5

The Locating of Data (Where They Are)

In programming for a microprocessor at the assembly language level, more than for larger machines, it is necessary to be highly conscious of the physical inter-relationships among the components of the machine. While this may seem to present even more of a burden for learning an assembly language, it is in fact a means by which to simplify enormously the whole learning process. Once one is aware of how the various data-storing modules of the processor are related one to the other, the many pieces of the instruction set fall neatly together into families that are easily mastered. Chapter 7 will systematically present data movement (we could call it *register transfers* just as well). For now we shall consider the various places form which the movements originate. The locations of origin are (1) immediate mode specification within instructions; (2) accumulator; (3) registers; (4) stack and stack pointer; (5) program counter; and (6) I/O ports.

One of the advantages of FORTRAN, COBOL, PL/1, and other high-level languages is that the programmer may ignore almost completely the peculiarities of the computing system with which he is working. To the extent that this is true, the high-level language programmer may dedicate all his energies to solution of the problem at hand. The only hindrance to a FORTRAN programmer in starting up on a system that is new to him will probably be the uniqueness of that system's job control language (JCL). Normally, the programmer need only learn (*copy* is a more accurate term) a dozen or so lines of JCL in order to make the new system run his FORTRAN programs properly. And even JCL does not deal with the hardware of the system any more deeply than at the configuration level, the sequence numbers of the mass storage devices, specification of user work areas, default, and requested maximum execution times, for example. Not only does this strategy promote a higher level of productivity among applications programmers individually, but it helps to assure a high level of portability of the software from system to system.

Real-time programs written for microprocessor systems, however, are typically written in the assembly language of the particular machine. (This trend is changing, and we include an appendix on PL/M for the 8080. But "real time," "microprocessor," and "assembler" are concepts that have compelling reasons for remaining tightly associated for some time to come.) As we have mentioned before, the two strongest motivations for selecting assembler language are (1) the capability offered to the programmer to encode algorithms into as few machine instructions as possible, thereby ensuring that each program will

43

execute in the minimum time possible and according to instruction times that are known directly by the programmer, (2) the guarantee that this minimum number of instructions will therefore require the least amount of memory per copy of the final microprocessor product, and (3) the cheaper cost of a stand-alone development system capable of compiling assembler code only. Such an assembler-only system typically requires far less memory than is necessary for a high-level language.

The tradeoff for the programmer of such a system is that he must learn a language that is peculiar to the computer with which he is working. Just how an assembly language evolves with its own peculiarities and its own unique instruction set for a particular computer is a history that is different for each machine and is beyond the scope of this book. But one thing is certain, the designers of the language did not sit down at some weekend retreat and invent the language *in vacuo*. The language evolves, is influenced by, and helps to influence the evolution of the architecture of the hardware itself. An assembly language therefore represents half the end product of an immense number of tradeoff considerations, the other half being the microprocessor itself.

Computer architecture is a vast study that we shall indulge in only by means of a perverse example. Most programmers would probably laud the advent of an assembly language instruction set that incorporated 15 (or 50 perhaps) general-purpose registers, each of which had direct access to the internal data bus and which therefore would ensure that a program would have to access memory only very infrequently. The only problem with such a system is that it would be difficult to fit physically onto a single chip; it certainly would have litttle room left to accomplish arithmetic and logical operations or to perform I/O. The point to remember, therefore, is that for microprocessors in particular, an assembly language is an intimate representation of the architecture of the machine for which it was designed.

The reason for this discussion is not only to encourage the reader to study computer architecture formally. There is also a pedagogical payoff here which will make learning the language much easier than would otherwise be possible. That is, rather than to grind laboriously through the instruction set in alphabetical order, or by some other contrived scheme, we shall present first a highly simplified, but faithful representation of the functional block description of the 8080 processor chip. (In this scheme, only registers and the arithmetic logic unit will be considered as the components.) We shall then see how the instruction set of the 8080 assembler falls out naturally from this architecture. In Chapter 7 we shall present in detail the families of instructions that are grouped according to this simplified structure.

8080 Architecture

Accumulator

(For each of the components of the processor, refer to Figure 5-1.) The name of this register is an unfortunate relic from the days of the earliest electronic

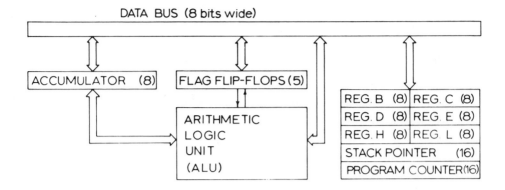

Figure 5-1. Simplified Block Diagram of 8080A Processor.

calculators. This register does more than just accumulate results during arithmetic calculations; it is far more versatile in nature, so much more active and versatile than the other registers that we shall enumerate shortly that it scarcely deserves to be called a mere *register*. Any term we use to describe it must begin with *A*, since the instruction set uses that letter. But we can assume any title we wish: *arch register, acme, activissimo*. The privileged position of the accumulator derives from its ability to communicate directly (as far as the programmer is concerned) with memory, with other registers, and even with data contained within instructions themselves. Just how this quality of superdirectness is manifested in the instruction set will be seen in detail in Chapter 7. For now, let us say simply that the accumulator can participate directly in an entire subset of the instructions of the 8080, performing activities that cannot be accomplished by the other registers.

Flags

There are five two-state switches (flip-flops) that convey single bits of information of critical importance to the programmer. Another name for this array of bits is *processor status word* (PSW). Occasionally the entire PSW is moved by the programmer, and under program control the individual bits can be toggled. Normally, however, the flags are only interrogated (read) the by user's program for decision-making purposes.

Registers

Yes, there really are six (count 'em) registers, in addition to the accumulator. They are all 8 bits "wide," and they can all be individual sources and destinations of data movement. But the reader will notice that the naming scheme for the registers is not overpowering in its aesthetic appeal. For now, note simply that B is somehow associated with C (A was used for *accumulator,* remember?), D goes with E, and H and L also belong together. It is not therefore profound to observe that these 6 registers are referred to as *register pairs.* In practice, the registers are anything but general purpose; the instruction set itself, as shall be seen in the next chapter, practically dictates the special purposes for each register pair.

Memory

We normally distinguish between *program,* residing in one portion of memory, and *data* (the stuff upon which the program operates), residing in another. (By *memory,* of course, we are referring not to peripheral device memory, such as on a disk or tape, but to the fast, on-board kind that is built into IC chips and addressed by the microprocessor directly.) We must remind ourselves that as far as the memory chips themselves are concerned, there need not be any physical difference between the program segment of memory and the data segment. (Of course, fully tested, production copies of programs are normally loaded once and for all into read-only memory, and data may reside in either read-only or random-access, read-write memory.) Because this is true, it is entirely possible for 8- or 16-bit length data to reside within individual instructions, provided that these data are to be read only. There is nothing so novel about this; it is taken for granted in high-level languages and in all assembler languages as well. Data that are accessed in this manner are said to be *immediate,* and the manner of its access is called *immediate mode.* We are emphasizing the point only because an entire segment of the 8080 instruction set is especially designated as *immediate-mode instructions,* and to realize the distinction enjoyed by immediate-mode data makes learning the instruction set much easier.

But the larger chunks of data which the program is to manipulate, such as lists, arrays, and other structures, cannot possibly be accessed in the immediate mode. Those data must reside in nonprogram portions of memory. And the instruction within the program that accesses those data can do so in one of two ways. First, the instruction may contain within itself the address of the data being referenced. This is called *direct-mode addressing,* because the address given within the instruction is the address of the data. We are emphasizing the meaning of *direct* here in order to clarify the possible semantic confusion between *immediate* and *direct.*

The second manner of referencing data in nonprogram memory is *indirectly,* through an address contained in registers, which themselves are contained within the instruction. Now let us review carefully the distinction between *immediate, direct,* and *indirect;* it will greatly simplify our attack on the instruction set:

1. Immediate-mode data reside within the instruction itself.
2. Direct-mode data are pointed to by an address contained within the instruction.
3. Indirect-mode data are pointed to by a register which is referenced within the instruction. For the 8080, the register pair is H,L and is designated as M when indirect referencing is desired.

```
1 MVI    B,OFEH      ;IMMEDIATE
2 MOV    B,DATA      ;DIRECT
3 MOV    B,M         ;INDIRECT
```

Stack and Stack Pointer

There is a special portion of memory whose chief function is to save and restore bytes of data within the user's program. For example, suppose that the programmer has just loaded registers B and C with some important data from memory, and now he must do something else with registers B and C without destroying their contents. He places ("pushes") the 2 bytes onto the stack, uses registers B and C for awhile, then restores ("pops") the original contents of B and C from the stack back to the registers. (Writers often refer to the spring-loaded stack of dishes in a cafeteria line to describe a program's stacking mechanism, but the spring may tend to confuse some readers.)

Because the stack is so special to the computer, there is a special two-word address register whose sole function is to point to the exact location in memory at which the next "pushed" word will reside; it is called the *stack pointer.* In a properly functioning program, the stack pointer can be relied upon to produce the proper data when the stack is "popped." All this should be intuitively obvious thus far. The only possible confusion results from the convention used in addressing the stack: the bottom of the stack has the highest address and the top has the lowest address. Put another way, each "push" onto the stack decrements the stack pointer, and each "pop" increments the stack pointer. Study the examples in Figure 5-2. As might be expected, there are instructions which pertain exclusively to the stack and stack pointer. For now, we are interested only in the stack pointer as a two-word register and the stack as a portion of memory, each of which can participate in the movement of data.

Program Counter

During the execution of a program, a portion of 8080 hardware is dedicated to deciphering each of the instructions and to resetting a pointer to the next instruction to be executed. That pointer is called the *program counter* and is

	PUSH B		POP B	
STACK AREA	BEFORE:	AFTER:	BEFORE:	AFTER:
1FFF	15	15	15	15
1FFE	C3	C3	C3	C3
1FFD	OB	A9	A9	A9
1FFC	E6	03	03	03
1FFB	24	24	24	24.
1FFA	18	18	18	18

STACK POINTER

1FFE	1FFC	1FFC	1FFE

REGISTER PAIR B,C

A9	03	A9	03	32	C6	A9	03

Figure 5-2. Effects of PUSH, POP Instructions.

naturally a very critical portion of the system. Because it must be able to locate any word in memory, it is 16 bits long. As with the stack pointer, the program counter will be considered a special-purpose register. And although it is accessed heavily by the hardware of the 8080 itself, it is accessible to the user via some special instructions in the assembly language. It is therefore one further participant in data movement among registers.

I/O Ports

All the registers and memory areas we have presented thus far are located either on the 8080 chip itself or within the memory accessed directly by the microprocessor. And the large majority of the instructions of the assembly language concern themselves with activity within these areas. But the most significant activity for applications is focused upon the 8080's communication with the outside world. For now we shall assume that either a byte to input to the processor or a byte to be output from the processor resides in a predetermined location in the hardware, called a *port,* either input or output. Although this sounds like a dishonest simplification, that is practically all that the programmer needs to know about interfacing through I/O ports. It is obviously a very powerful feature of the design of the 8080. Ports will be used in the design example later on.

Summary

As shall be indicated in Chapter 7, many of the instructions of the 8080 assembly language pertain to moving data: from register to register, from memory to registers, and from registers to memory. And, in fact, most of the coding done in the language will be done for accomplishing such movement. Therefore, since so much attention is given by the programmer to transfers, this chapter has attempted to provide some structure for learning the instructions. This is done by situating all possible sources and destinations of movement within the total landscape.

Exercises

5-1. Summarize the three modes of addressing possible with the 8080. Can you spot examples of two of the modes in the programs reproduced in Chapter 13? Discuss immediate-mode addressing from the dual standpoint of (a) readability and (b) modifiability (maintenance) of the code.

5-2. Describe in your own words the function of each of the following "data-holding structures" (registers) in the 8080: (a) accumulator; (b) PC; (c) SP; (d) PSW; and (e) other registers.

5-3. Consult the data guide (printed specifications and block diagrams) published by the manufacturer of a microprocessor other than the 8080. Find the components mentioned in question 5-2 for the 8080 in the architecture of the other microprocessor, if they exist.

6 Organizing Data in Memory (How to Put Them There)

Programmers who prefer to work with assembly languages as opposed to high-level languages say such things as "with an assembler, you know *exactly* what you're doing! You know what is happening at each step, since you are doing it all yourself." And that same sentiment applies to the programmer's manipulation of data using an assembler. There is no way for the programmer, for example, to call out "array," giving some dimensions, and then expect that the program will understand what "the element in the *i*th row and the *j*th column" is equal to. It is the assembly language programmer's total responsibility to keep track of the nature of each structure, whether that structure is a single-byte-length variable, a single-dimensional array, or a table (a two-dimensional array), and whether the value in a particular memory location is to be treated as a variable in its own right or as an address of still another location.

The maintenance of data structures in user (fast) memory frequently occupies much of the programmer's attention in real-time applications. There are typically no mass storage devices in which data have already been laid out in some prescribed format. Rather, the real-time system will generally be reading from structures that reside in read-only memory (ROM) and then constantly updating structures in read-write memory (most frequently called *random-access memory,* or RAM). A heavy amount of in-line (sequential instruction) code can be saved by relying on carefully designed data structures. And in applications requiring that a single processor service more than one device (both a keyboard and the serializer interface of a remote terminal, for example), the use of data structures is absolutely essential.

The good news for assembly language programmers is not only that they always know what each instruction is doing, but that setting up data structures requires very little (and very simple) coding. As a point of semantics, we say that we *direct* the compiler to allocate memory in the way we prescribe. The set of such specifications for a language is called the *assembler directives* for that language. (The total set of assembler directives accomplishes much more than memory layout, but we are only interested in memory at the moment.) The formal distinction between an instruction and a directive is that an instruction, on one hand, is first assembled (compiled) into something executable by a particular machine and is executed each time the assembled program is run. An assembler directive, on the other hand, is given by the programmer directly to the assembler and provides vital information as to how the program is to be compiled in the first place. Or, we may say that a directive is executed once

51

only, at *compile time,* while an instruction is executed at *run time,* every time the program is run. Let us discuss briefly now the assembler directives that are needed for the 8080 programmer to specify all the structures necessary to a typical real-time application. In the last chapter, we alluded to data that resided in the processor's memory, but outside the actual program area of memory. When programmers refer to *resident data,* they are referring to this mode of data residency.

Now, let us structure this discussion around the three tasks that must be accomplished relative to the layout of user memory: (1) the definition of symbols; (2) the definition of user data; and (3) the reservation of memory.

Defining Symbols

When a FORTRAN programmer uses symbols, as in GO TO 10 or PROFIT = .05 GROSS (in which 10, PROFIT, and GROSS are symbols), he or she may not be aware that some mechanism was necessary to make each of the symbols recognizable and meaningful to the program as a whole. That mechanism creates what for nearly every language is called a *symbol table,* something that is normally very transparent to the programmer. For the 8080 there are basically two ways to cause something to be entered into the symbol table: as an instruction label or as a programmer-defined symbol.

Instruction Label

This is the most automatic way of defining a symbol. Whenever the programmer places a label in the leftmost field of an instruction, the assembler recognizes that label as a symbol and enters the label, together with its location, into the symbol table.

```
LOOP01:   LXI    D,'AB'    ;LOAD ASCII CODE FOR 'A' AND
                           ; 'B' INTO REGISTERS D AND E
```

Note that there is a colon following the label.

Programmer-Defined Symbol

There are two directives in the 8080 assembler for defining symbols under programmer control: EQU and SET. EQU is a compile-time assignment operator that is "once and for all":

```
LOMASK    EQU    OFH    ;LET LOMASK = 00001111
HIMASK    EQU    FOH    ;LET HIMASK = 11110000
```

Note that there is no colon following the symbol that is being defined in this manner. Wherever LOMASK or HIMASK occurs in the program, the symbol table (which incorporated these symbols from the directive) is referred to for the proper value to be assigned.

SET

This directive accomplishes the same thing for a symbol as does EQU, but a subsequent SET directive (i.e., further along in the program, as it is being compiled) may reassign a value to the symbol. This virtually allows the programmer repeated access to the symbol itself for purposes of altering its value at will. For example, suppose that the symbol FREQ is used to determine how frequently a light on a clinical instrument's display panel is to flash alternatively on and off, in case of decreased arterial blood pressure. The lower the pressure, beyond a certain threshold, the more rapid is to be the alternation of the alarm light (or audible signal). If the signal symbol FREQ is used to govern this frequency, then it would be useful to be able to alter its value under program control.

```
FREQ   SET    60     ;60 ALTERNATIONS/MINUTE
FREQ   SET    80     ;80 ALTERNATIONS/MINUTE
```

Defining User Data

There are two directives for allocating and initializing user data, one for defining the data by bytes (DB) and the other for word-length (2-byte) units (DW).

It is important to note first that the *values* which are specified in the DB and DW directives are specified for the exact location within the code in which they appear; these are not definitions in the symbol table. Second, not every byte location needs to be labeled; a single label may point to a series of DB directives. Study the following pair of data lists:

```
BYTABL:                    ;TABLE OF BYTE-LENGTH
                           ; NUMBERS
          DB     1
          DB     2
          DB     3
          DB     4
     ;
     ; NOTE THAT THE SINGLE LABEL POINTS TO THE
     ; HEAD OF THE ENTIRE LIST.
     ;
```

```
WDTABL:                    ;TABLE OF WORD-LENGTH
                           ; NUMBERS
          DW      1
          DW      2
          DW      3
          DW      4

DB
```

For each DB directive, note the effect on program memory, as shown in Figure 6-1. This list of definitions initializes a series of byte locations in memory, beginning at the location of the label DAYS. This is an example of defining bytes with strings, in which ASCII values are automatically substituted for string characters, one by one, byte by byte.

Naturally, a numeric expression may be used as the value to be assigned, for example:

```
NULL:     DB      00H           ;BYTE LOCATION "NULL" = 0
CMPLEX:   DB      3*4           ;HEX C STORED AT "CMPLEX"
LIST:     DB      5-2,4,0AH,10  ;4 ASSORTED BYTE VALUES
```

One may wonder whether the value to be assigned by DB to a byte location may itself be a pointer (address) to another byte. The answer is no in the case of the DB directive, inasmuch as both symbols and other addressed memory locations must be 2 bytes long. (Such assignments can be, and are, frequently made for whole words. As shall be seen in the discussion of DW.)

The reader may have read rather quickly over the example above with NULL. This example was included out of sheer malice aforethought. The reason is to remind you of what you are doing when you represent symbols and variables. We said previously that a label is a type of symbol that has some value assigned automatically by the compiler. In the compiler sense, therefore, it must be realized that the value of NULL (as a label within the user's memory area) is the *address* at which that label appears. In this case, the address would be expressed using some hexadecimal number, (CAAH for example). But the value of NULL is not 00H! It is only in the applications sense, when the technicalities of addressing are ignored for convenience in problem solving, that it is said that "the value of NULL is zero". In actual programming practice within the 8080, however, we must always be aware that a memory location is accessed through an address. The label name we pick to represent a variable in our particular program has as its value an address of a memory location containing some value we have assigned to that variable.

```
LOC  OBJ      SEQ     SOURCE STATEMENT

                1  ; EXAMPLES OF "DB" AND "DW" ASSEMBLER DIRECTIVES
                2  ;
                3  BYTABL:              ;TABLE OF BYTE-LENGTH NUMBERS
0000 01         4        DB    1
0001 02         5        DB    2
0002 03         6        DB    3
0003 04         7        DB    4
0004 05         8        DB    5,6,7,8,9,10
0005 06
0006 07
0007 08
0008 09
0009 0A

                9
000A 0100      10  WDTABLE:             ;TABLE OF WORD-LENGTH NUMBERS
000C 0200      11        DW    1
000E 0300      12        DW    2
0010 0400      13        DW    3
0012 0500      14        DW    4,5,10,12
0014 0A00
0016 0C00

               15
0018 53554E    16  DAYS:                ;ASCII CHARACTER TABLE (BYTES)
001B 4D4F4E    17        DB    'SUN'
001E 54554553  18        DB    'MON'
0022 574544    19        DB    'TUES'
0025 54485552  20        DB    'WED'
0029 53        21        DB    'THURS'
002A 465249    22        DB    'FRI'
002D 534154    23        DB    'SAT'

               24
0030 414A      25  MONTHS:              ;ASCII TABLE (WORDS)
0032 4546      26        DW    'JA'     ;(ONLY UP TO TWO CHARACTERS ALLOWED PER STRING)
0034 414D      27        DW    'FE'
0036 5041      28        DW    'MA','AP','MY'
0038 594D

               29
               30  END
```

PUBLIC SYMBOLS

EXTERNAL SYMBOLS

USER SYMBOLS
BYTABL A 0000   DAYS   A 0018   MONTHS A 0030   WDTABL A 000A

ASSEMBLY COMPLETE,   NO ERRORS

Figure 6-1. Examples of DB, DW Assembler Directives.

DW

The operation of the DW directive is what we should expect: assign whole word (2-byte) values instead of single bytes. But this can in turn cause us some confusion, since we are dealing with an 8-bit and not a 16-bit machine. The important point (and this sounds trivial) is that the least significant 8 bits of the word (expression or string) go into the first byte and the most significant bits go into the next byte. Let us now study some examples which utilize the DW directive. We shall point out some potential pitfalls (particularly in the case of ASCII strings). Study Figure 6-1 carefully, noting especially the layout of the memory. Based on these examples, the following may be observed:

1. Values in the operand field may be specified in any format: hexadecimal, decimal, octal, binary, or ASCII.
2. For a numeric expression, the low-order byte in memory corresponds to the arithmetic low-order portion of the number.
3. The value to be loaded may be a 16-bit address, low-order 8 bits first (see USER SYMBOLS in the example).
4. The value may be an ASCII string, specified to the assembler by means of single quotes. (See DAYS in the listing.) String definitions by DW have the following properties: the length of each string may be 1 or 2 only; for strings only, left is low (in MONTHS, the J of JA is first (= 4A hex)); for single-byte strings in DW definitions, the ASCII field is "right-justified," a zero being automatically inserted in the high-order byte.
5. A list of items (up to eight), separated by commas, may be included in a single operand.
6. Expressions may include arithmetic operators to determine values to be assigned. Note that the integer division throws away the remainder.

Defining User Read-Write Space

The important directive DS designates the number of bytes in read-write memory to be assigned to begin at a particular labeled location, as follows:

```
BUFFER:   DS     150      ;150 BYTES' WORTH OF SPACE
```

Note that this assumes nothing about the contents of BUFFER. The directive merely allocates the memory area; it does not initialize it.

Memory Layout

Not only must a real-time programmer be highly conscious of individual data elements and data structures as they are laid out in memory, but he or she must also plan from the outset just how memory as a whole is to be mapped. We are thinking here primarily about starting locations: of instructions, of data structures, of the stack and stack pointer, and (as shall be presented later) of interrupt-servicing code. (We should mention here that microprocessor development systems allow great programmer flexibility, with very little learning effort, in the area of memory management. We shall therefore leave this for the reader to pursue through reading about linking and related topics in the particular development system manuals.)

In a typical real-time design situation, the programmer will be told that memory will be limited to a given amount, say 8K bytes. Moreover, it might be specified that the total amount will be divided, say, between 4K of ROM (read-only memory, which is relatively cheap when considered for large-scale production), and 4K of RAM (random-access memory, which is relatively more costly).

The implication of this for the programmer of our system is that the executable instructions and initialized, read-only data structures (defined by DW and DB) must be forced into the 4K of ROM (locations 0000H to 0FFFH), while the read-write data structures and the stack area must reside in the 4K of RAM (1000H to 1FFFH). Furthermore, the first 3 FH bytes of ROM are to be reserved for interrupt-service routines (a topic that was investigated in Chapter 2). This "memory mapping" is depicted in Figure 6-2. Note from the map that the start of the stack is the highest address in memory. Pushing items onto the stack causes its pointer to be decremented.

We should be delighted to learn that accomplishing all this is trivial from a coding standpoint, involving only two assembler directives, plus one instruction:

```
ORG         0040H     ;START OF PROGRAM IN ROM
PROGRM:     . . . .    ;
            LXI        ;SP ,01FFFH ;SET STACK POINTER → TOP
            . . . .    ; OF RAM

            . . . .
R.WDAT:     ORG        1000H     ;START OF READ/WRITE DATA
```

The directive ORG forces the location pointers to the memory locations indicated. At the start of PROGRM, therefore, (at which PROGRM will be the labeled entry point of the code) the assembler will automatically assign the address 40H to the first instruction. The mnemonic SP refers to the stack pointer, which is being initialized.

58

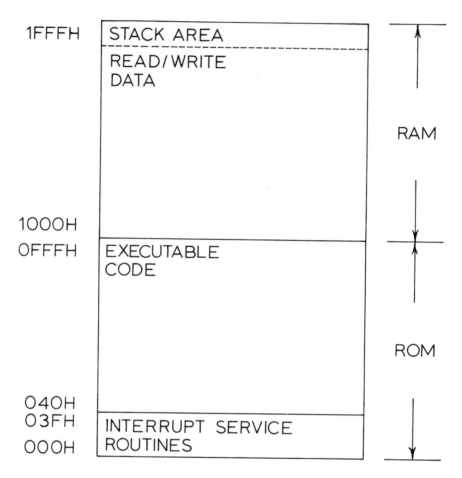

Figure 6-2. Layout (Mapping) of 8K of Memory.

Exercises

6-1. Discuss three ways to enter symbols into the symbol table for a program.

6-2. a. Use 8080 assembler code to define masks (as symbols) for bits 0–3. b. Define a loop count initialization symbol having the value 60 (decimal).

6-3. Since it is possible to include algebraic expressions with previously defined symbols within other symbol definitions, define a loop counter that is three times the value of the one in question 6-2b.

6-4. A particular loop is known to take LOPTIM microseconds to execute, and LOPTIM is defined at the start of the program as a symbol. Assuming that TOTDLY is also defined (as a symbol) to be the total number of microseconds required for a particular delay, use an algebraic expression within the symbol definition for ITERAT, the number times that the loop should be executed.

6-5. Define the space required for DEVTBL, a device table with necessary characteristics for several devices controlled by the microprocessor. Each entry will be 4 bytes wide, and there will be five entries in the table.

6-6. Use the DB directive only to define and initialize (to zero) the same table as in question 6-5.

7

Manipulating Data: Transfers

Having observed in a general manner the possible locations of data, we are now prepared to consider the functions that the various instructions of the assembly language perform. We discover that the entire instruction set can be reduced to only three major functions: movement (transfers), logical operations, and calculations. In this chapter, we shall restrict the scope to individual instructions. We shall determine what happens to each entity concerned *within* the particular instruction.

There is no clean demarcation between high-level and low-level software or even between software and hardware. We are therefore justified in considering the entire spectrum in our discussion. So it is that while only a limited number of software instructions appear to be moves in the high-level sense, at the flip-flop level of the hardware all the possible instructions can be considered as register transfers. That observation is a bit too theoretical to be applied directly to programming, but it helps to explain why much of the assembly language programmer's time is spent in writing code that simply moves data from one location to another, a byte or word at a time. Since this is true, we shall concentrate heavily on all the possible move instructions, implied or expressed, in order that the reader may gain total "fluency" in this most important area of language activity.

The plan of attack is first to "consider the source" of each transfer. And we shall divide the discussion between single-byte and double-byte transfers.

A word about format: The instructions for the 8080 (as finally compiled) vary in total length from 1 to 3 bytes. Instructions in the source code likewise vary in number of fields, from 1 to 3, the first always being the "op code" itself. In the description, the mnemonic op code will appear in the first field. Any fields that have options to choose from will be indicated with braces. When any item in a particular field is spelled with capital letter(s), then that exact spelling must be used in the instruction. When a parameter is spelled with lower case letters, then that lower case spelling is simply a description of what must really be inserted in that field of the instruction.

Single-Byte Transfers

1. From Immediate Data

To a Register (A,B,C,D,E,H, or L).

61

$$\text{MVI} \quad \begin{Bmatrix} \text{A} \\ \text{B} \\ \text{C} \\ \text{D} \\ \text{E} \\ \text{H} \\ \text{L} \end{Bmatrix} \quad , data$$

Since this same list of register options will be referred to so frequently, we shall use the coded abbreviation *reg* to refer to that list and only that list. For some instructions, only a subset of that list is possible, and in these cases, the actual list of all possible registers will be spelled out in full; for example:

```
MVI    A,64           ;MOVE 64 (DECIMAL) INTO
                      ; ACCUMULATOR
MVI    A,01000000B    ;EQUIVALENT TO ABOVE
MVI    A,100Q         ;EQUIVALENT AGAIN
MVI    E,32           ;MOVE 32 INTO REG. E
```

To Memory. Immediate data are moved to memory via an indirect reference to memory, and that reference is set up as follows. First the H,L register pair (considered now as a single, 16-bit unit) is loaded with the address of the memory to which the immediate data are to be moved. Now, with H,L properly loaded (by the user in some previous instruction), that memory location is specified in the MVI instruction simply by the letter M. M is not the name of any register; it is rather a shorthand method of saying "the memory location currently pointed to the H,L register pair." This use of M will be precisely the same for all environments within which it is used.

The format for the MVI instruction for moving an immediate data byte to memory is:

```
MVI    M,data
```

Data represents any of the proper numeric forms, as described in Chapter 4; for example

```
MVI    M,0AH          ;MOVE 0A HEX TO MEMORY
                      ; LOCATION SPECIFIED
                      ; IN H,L REGISTER PAIR
MVI    M,120Q         ;MOVE 120 OCTAL LIKEWISE
```

2. From the Accumulator

To a Register (including itself).

```
MOV     reg,A
```

For example:

```
MOV     D,A     ;MOVE CONTENTS OF ACCUMULATOR
                ; TO REG. D
```

To Memory.
1. Direct addressing:

```
STA     address
```

For example:

```
STA     TABLE   ;PLACE CONTENTS OF ACCUMULATOR
                ; AT MEMORY LOCATION LABELED
                ; "TABLE"
STA     600H    ;STORE CONTENTS AT MEMORY
                ; LOCATION 600 HEX
```

2. Indirect addressing:

```
STAX    { B }   ;PUT CONTENTS INTO LOCATION
        { D }   ; SPECIFIED BY REGISTER PAIR
                : B,C OR D,E
```

For example:

```
STAX    B       ;MOVE CONTENTS OF ACCUMULATOR
                ; TO MEMORY ADDRESS NOW RESIDING
                ; IN REGISTER PAIR B,C
```

Notes on STAX: X in the op code refers to *register pair* (B,C or D,E). The memory address must be a full 16 bits in length. Hence, the entire register pair must be used. This instruction assumes that the user has previously loaded a proper memory address into the register pair selected. The register pair H,L is not legal in this instruction. H,L *is* used for this purpose in a plain MOV instruction, which moves data from any register, including the accumulator. This will be covered in the upcoming discussion on registers.

To Itself, Altered.
1. Rotate accumulator right:
    RAR: *through carry bit.* The accumulator is rotated right one bit position, and the carry flag bit participates in the rotation between the high and low bits of the accumulator (study Figure 7–1a).

ACCUMULATOR   CARRY

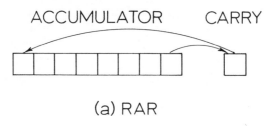

(a) RAR

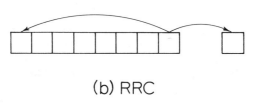

(b) RRC

Note: RAR rotates a bit through CARRY; RRC does not (the mnemonics are confusing).
Figure 7-1. Effects of ROTATE Instructions.

RRC: *set carry equal to least significant bit of accumulator.* In this rotate instruction, the least significant bit is rotated directly into the most significant bit, while the carry flag bit is simply set equal to the least significant bit of the accumulator (study the contrast between Figures 7-1a and b).

2. Rotate accumulator left:
    RAL: *through the carry bit.* Same as for RAR, except for direction.
    RLC: same as for RRC, except for direction.
Note: be sure to master the diagrams thoroughly, inasmuch as the op code mnemonics are misleading.

3. Complement accumulator:
    CMA: complement (invert) each bit of the accumulator.

To Output Ports.

    OUT   *port number*

OUT moves the accumulator to the output port specified. (The number is purely a function of the particular hardware configuration and need not concern us here.)

In these instructions we have observed some special qualities of the accumulator: (1) it is the only register whose contents can be moved to memory via direct addressing (STA); (2) it is the only register whose contents can be moved to memory via indirect referencing by register pairs other than the H,L pair (STAX); (3) it is the only register than can be rotated; and (4) it is the only register connecting directly with I/O ports (OUT).

3. From a Register (any *reg* as a data source, including the accumulator)

To a Register (including itself and the accumulator).

```
MOV     reg2,reg1       ;MOVE CONTENTS OF reg1 TO reg2
```

For example:

```
MOV     H,A       ;MOVE ACCUMULATOR TO REG H
```

To Memory.

```
MOV     M,reg     ;MOVE reg TO LOCATION
                  ; SPECIFIED BY H,L PAIR
```

For example:

```
MOV     M,B       ;MOVE B TO LOCATION IN H,L
MOV     M,A       ;MOVE A TO LOCATION IN H,L
```

4. From Memory (any byte in memory as a data source)

To the Accumulator.
1. Direct addressing:

```
LDA     address   ;MOVE CONTENTS OF address
                  ; TO ACCUMULATOR
```

For examples:

```
LDA     05AAH        ;MOVE BYTE STORED AT LOCATION
                     ; 5AA TO ACCUMULATOR
LDA     SOURCE       ;FETCH BYTE FROM MEMORY LOCATION
                     ; LABELED "SOURCE" AND DEPOSIT
                     ; IN ACCUMULATOR
```

2. Indirect addressing:

```
LDAX     {B}     ;LOAD BYTE STORED AT LOCATION
         {D}     ; SPECIFIED BY PAIR B,C OR D,E
                 ; INTO ACCUMULATOR
```

For example:

```
LDAX     D       ;LOAD ACCUMULATOR WITH CONTENTS
                 ; OF MEMORY LOCATION SPECIFIED
                 ; BY REGISTER PAIR D,E
```

See notes following **STAX** above; they are all pertinent to **LDAX** as well.

To any Register (including the accumulator).

```
MOV      reg,M   ;MOVE BYTE STORED AT LOCATION
                 ; ADDRESSED BY H,L INTO SINGLE
                 ; REGISTER reg
```

For example:

```
MOV      E,M     ;MOVE BYTE ADDRESSED BY H,L INTO E
```

5. From I/O Ports (as sources)

To Accumulator (only destination possible).

```
IN       nnnn    ;MOVE THE BYTE AT ADDRESS nnnn
                 ; TO THE ACCUMULATOR
```

The address nnnn is predetermined by the particular hardware configuration of which this microprocessor is a part.

This concludes the discussion of data transfers of single bytes, listed according to all possible sources. Table 7–1 summarizes the discussion. And finally, Figure 7–2 is a graphical equivalent of the same information, in which each of the possible data sources are represented by nodes and each of the possible transfer instructions are shown as directed arcs connecting the nodes.

Double-Byte Transfers

As in the case of single-byte data transfers, double-byte transfers will be considered according to all possible sources from which double-byte data can

Table 7–1
Single-Byte Register Transfers

Source	Destination	Instruction Format
1. Immediate data	Register	MVI *reg, data*
	Memory	MVI M, *data*
2. Accumulator	Register	MOV *reg*, A
	Memory	STA *address*
		(MOV M, A)
	I/O port	OUT *port number*
3. Other register (B, C, D, E, H, L)	Register	MOV *reg, reg*
	Memory	MOV M, *reg*
4. Memory	Accumulator	LDA *address*
		(MOV A, M)
	Other register	MOV *reg*, M
5. I/O port	Accumulator	IN *port number*

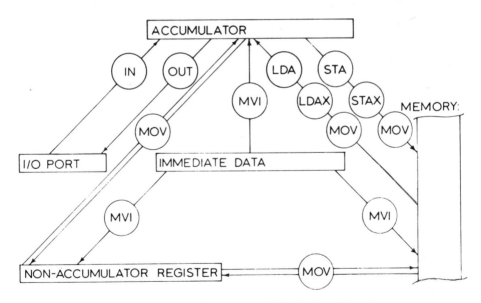

Figure 7-2. Graphical Summary of Single-Byte Transfers.

originate. The list of sources is as follows: (1) immediate data; (2) register pair (B,C; D,E; H,L; SP; PSW (= A, *status flags*)); (3) H,L; (4) D,E; (5) stack (top 2 bytes); and (6) memory. Although it may appear redundant for items 3 through 5 to be included also as part of item 2, we shall point out later that each of the numbered items comprises a unique source that helps us to categorize the double-byte instructions. Let us therefore approach these instructions in the order specified in the preceding list.

1. From immediate data to a register pair (the only destination possible for double-byte immediate data)

LXI $\begin{Bmatrix} B \\ D \\ H \end{Bmatrix}$,*data*   ;MOVE THE SIXTEEN-BIT *data*
                 ; INTO THE REGISTER PAIR

For example:

LXI	H,MEMLOC	;SET H,L POINTING TO MEMORY ; LOCATION "MEMLOC" (LABEL ; OR USER-DEFINED SYMBOL)
LXI	B,'HI'	;MOVE ASCII 'H' INTO B, 'I' INTO ; C
LXI	B,4849H	;SAME AS ABOVE (HEX ; EQUIVALENT)
LXI	B0100100001001001B	;SAME AGAIN (BINARY)

2. To register pair (B,D,H,SP,PSW)

This group of register pairs, considered as a group, has only a single possible destination, the top of the stack:

PUSH $\begin{Bmatrix} B \\ D \\ H \\ PSW \end{Bmatrix}$

When a PUSH instruction is executed, three different entities of data are affected, and the hardware of the microprocessor assists to accomplish the following. First, the 16 bits of data contained in the register pair are moved into the location in the stack pointed to by the stack pointer. This is accomplished as follows: (1) the first register (B, D, H, or A) is moved into the "topmost" location of the stack, and (2) the second register (C, E, L, or flags) is moved into the next byte location of the stack. Second, the value contained in the stack pointer (SP) is decremented by two (one for each byte location used in the stack). Study Figure 5-2 again to trace the preceding sequence of events.

3. From H,L *Register Pair Only*

For H,L only there are two possible destinations, plus two possible exchanges with other double-byte data.

To a Memory Location.

    SHLD   *addr*   ;STORE H,L AT *addr* SPECIFIED DIRECTLY

For example:

    SHLD   STRLOC   ;STORE CONTENTS OF H,L AT STRLOC+1
                                  ; AND STRLOC, RESPECTIVELY

The possible pitfall in this instruction is that H really means "high byte" and L means "low byte". This means that in looking at the referenced memory location following the instruction we will find the contents of L first (at STRLOC) and H second (at STRLOC+1).

To the stack pointer.

    SPHL   ;MOVE H,L INTO STACK POINTER

In view of the criticality of the stack and stack pointer, it would seem risky to tamper with the stack pointer, and so it is. But when its value must be changed, here is the only way it can be done under program control.

Exchange H,L **with the Topmost Bytes of Stack.**

    XTHL

This powerful instruction, with nothing besides the op code, actually swaps a double byte in the register pair H,L with the top 2 bytes on the stack.

Exchange H,L **with** D,E.

    XCHG   ;SWAP H,L WITH D,E

4. From D,E *Register Pair Only*

The only double-byte transfer possible is actually a swap with H,L.

    XCHG   ;SWAP D,E WITH H,L

5. *From Stack*

Considering the top 2 bytes of the stack as the source, there is one set of destinations and one swap possible in the instruction set.

To a Register Pair (B,C; D,E; H,L; PSW (= A, flags)).

POP $\left\{\begin{array}{c} B \\ D \\ H \\ PSW \end{array}\right\}$;MOVE TOPMOST TWO BYTES OF STACK
; INTO REGISTER PAIR SPECIFIED AND
; INCREMENT SP

For example:

```
POP     H       ;MOVE TOPMOST BYTE INTO L, NEXT
                ; HIGHEST INTO H, ADJUSTING SP
POP     PSW     ;MOVE TOPMOST BYTE INTO A, NEXT
                ; INTO FLAGS
```

The blow-by-blow description for POP is the opposite of that for PUSH: (1) the topmost word of the stack is moved into the low-order register; (2) the next byte on the stack is moved into the high-order register; and (3) the stack pointer is incremented by two, so that the next reference to the stack will point to the proper byte. (The increment is done automatically by the processor when POP is executed.)

Swap with H,L.

```
XTHL        ;EXCHANGE TOPMOST TWO BYTES OF STACK
            ; WITH H,L PAIR
```

6. *From Memory*

A double-byte segment of data in memory can be loaded directly only into the H,L pair.

```
LHLD    address     ;LOAD H,L FROM MEMORY
                    ; LOCATION ADDRESSED
```

For example:

```
LHLD    05AAH       ;MOVE BYTE AT LOCATION 5AA (HEX)
                    ; INTO L, BYTE AT 5AB INTO H
LHLD    DBLWRD      ;MOVE BYTE AT DBLWRD INTO L,
                    ; BYTE AT DBLWRD+1 INTO H
```

As the reader can see, the variety of data transfers allowed for double bytes is much more restricted than for single bytes. In Table 7-2 observe that all nine of the instructions cited implicitly specify (or may optionally specify) the H,L pair. And this seems logical, when we consider that H,L are used constantly as the implicit memory pointer (whenever the operand M is used to specify a memory location.)

As we did for the single-byte transfers, we include a graph (Figure 7-3) depicting the possible double-byte transfers, with a node for each possible source and a directed arc for each instruction. Register exchanges (swaps) are depicted as bidirectional, double-lined arcs.

Table 7-2
Double-Byte Register Transfers

Source	Destination	Instruction Format	
1. Immediate data	B, C	LXI	B
	D, E	LXI	D
	H, L	LXI	H
	SP	LXI	SP
2. Register pair			
B, C	Top of stack	PUSH	B
D, E	Top of stack	PUSH	D
H, L	Top of stack	PUSH	H
PSW (= A, flags)	Top of stack	PUSH	PSW
3. H, L	Memory	SHLD	address
H, L	SP	SPHL	
H, L	PC	PCHL	
H, L	Top of stack (swap)	XTHL	
H, L	D, E (swap)	XCHG	
4. D, E	H, L (swap)	XCHG	
5. Top of stack	B, C	POP	B
Top of stack	D, E	POP	D
Top of stack	H, L	POP	H
Top of stack	PSW (= A, flags)	POP	PSW
Top of stack	H, L (swap)	XTHL	
6. Memory	H, L	LHLD	address

72

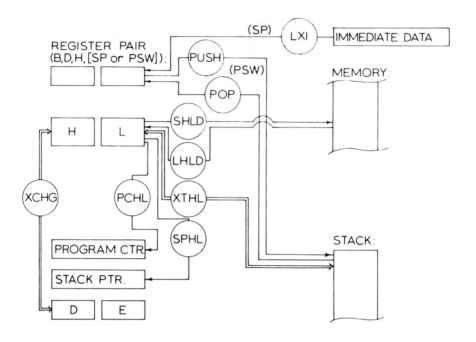

Note: The double-lined bidirectional paths represent swaps.

Figure 7–3. Graphical Summary of Word (Double-Byte) Transfers.

Exercises

For these coding exercises, refer to the origin-destination charts in this chapter.

7-1. Deposit the value 49 (decimal) into the accumulator. Assume that 49 is included within the instruction (immediate mode). Now rewrite the instruction for each of the other three numbering systems.

7-2. Now deposit 0FH into the memory location DATSAV (already defined as a labeled memory location), and rewrite the instruction for each of the other number bases.

7-3. Load the immediate data 128 (decimal) into the register pair B,C. Write the instruction once for each of the four numbering systems.

8

Manipulating Data: Logical Operations

Of all the types of activity in real-time programs, there is perhaps none so critical as that of testing, setting, and clearing bits in control/status registers. This is accomplished by means of the family of operations known as *logical operations.* However complicated a digital system may be, ultimately it may be viewed as a collection of primitive binary logical operations, with 2 input bits operated on in such a manner as to produce a single logical result or output. A convenient method for studying the logical results of all possible binary inputs is the truth table. Figure 8-1 contains the truth tables for AND, OR, and EXCLUSIVE-OR. (We are ignoring for the moment the particular op code mnemonics used for the 8080.) It is imperative to understand and to master these operations thoroughly. In the case of AND, the truth table may be paraphrased as follows:

1. If we AND a 0 and a 0, the result is 0.
2. If we AND a 0 and a 1, the result is 0.
3. If we AND a 1 and a 0, the result is 0.
4. If we AND a 1 and a 1, the result is 1.

The other tables may be "translated" in the same manner.

In order to "feel" more intuitively what each of the three logical operations accomplishes, it may help to paraphrase them as follows:

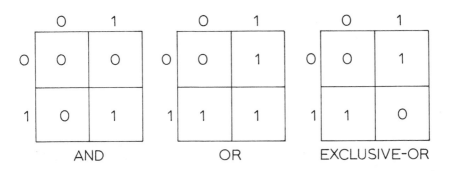

Figure 8-1. Truth Tables for AND, OR, EXCLUSIVE-OR Operations.

75

1. AND. Do both bits equal 1?
2. OR. Is either bit equal to 1?
3. EXCLUSIVE-OR. Is one and only one bit equal to 1?

So much for a single-bit pair. When considering more than one pair of bits, say eight pairs, simply apply the particular truth table to each pair, one "column" at a time. Let us convince ourselves of this by examining various register configurations as they are logically masked with the accumulator. The reader should be certain that he agrees with each bit of the result of each operation, as shown in Table 8-1. (The result is left in the accumulator after each operation.) Consider the effect of the bit mask on the contents of the accumulator (in Table 8-1) for each of the logical operations:

1. AND. A 0 in the mask *clears* a bit in the accumulator, a 1 leaves the accumulator bit *unchanged*.
2. OR. A 1 in the mask *sets* a bit in the accumulator, a 0 in the mask leaves the accumulator bit *unchanged*.
3. EXCLUSIVE-OR. A 1 in the mask *sets* a bit in the accumulator if that bit is *clear;* a 1 in the mask *clears* a bit in the accumulator if that bit is *set;* a 0 in the mask leaves the accumulator bit *unchanged.* In other words, a bit set in the mask toggles a bit in the accumulator.

The Plan of Attack: Consider the Mask

In the case of data transfers, we were able to structure the discussion of the instruction set by reference to the various sources of the transfers. Although the logical operations are much easier to keep tidy in our minds, we shall structure the discussion in this chapter according to the possible mask source: immediate data, single register, or byte in memory.

Immediate Data

$$
\left\{
\begin{array}{l}
\text{ANI} \\
\text{ORI} \\
\text{XRI} \\
\text{CPI}
\end{array}
\right\} \quad data \quad
\begin{array}{l}
\text{;AND IMMEDIATE DATA WITH ACCUMULATOR} \\
\text{;OR} \\
\text{;EXCLUSIVE-OR} \\
\text{;COMPARE}
\end{array}
$$

For purposes of bit manipulation, ANI, ORI, and XRI work on bits in the accumulator, as described in the previous section. For testing, either ANI (for interrogating individual bits within the accumulator and then looking at the Z flag) or CPI (for testing the whole accumulator and then checking the Z and

Table 8-1
Effect of Logical Operations on Accumulator

	AND:	OR:	XOR:
Mask:	10011100	10011100	10011100
Accumulator:	01110101	01110101	01110101
Result:	00010100	11111101	11101001

the C flags) are used. In the next chapter we shall point out how the programmer uses the flags, as set or cleared during logical operations, to direct the execution of a program properly.

Registers

```
(AND)   (A)
(ORA)   (B)   ;AND THE DATA IN REG WITH ACCUM
(XRA)   (C)   ;OR
(CMP)   (D)   ;EXCLUSIVE-OR
        (E)   ;COMPARE
        (H)
        (L)
```

Once again, note that the "destination" (i.e., the data being operated upon by the mask) resides in the accumulator. Note too that the final result of the logical operation (bits cleared, set, or toggled) is always in the accumulator. The accumulator, therefore, is a sort of "double destination." (In a later chapter we shall survey the effects of simply testing bits.)

Memory

As in the case of the data transfers, the use of M assumes that the register pair H,L has been properly loaded with a memory address. Thus, whenever M is used, what is meant is "the byte in memory addressed by the H,L register pairs."

```
(ANA)        ;AND MEMORY BYTE WITH ACCUMULATOR
(ORA)   M    ;OR
(XRA)        ;EXCLUSIVE-OR
(CMP)        ;COMPARE
```

Effect of Logical Operations on the Flags

In our description of the various components of the 8080 processor chip, we mentioned only that there is an array of five flags which comprise the register we call, simply, "the flags." (Other systems commonly speak of "status bits" which comprise a "processor status word." We have, in fact, already pointed out how the acronym PSW is used to refer to the accumulator and the flags taken together as a register pair in double-word transfers.) Although we defined all the flags at that time, we shall concentrate here on only two of these flags, the ones we shall utilize to direct program execution: the *zero* flag and the *carry* flag.

It may be helpful to gain a feeling for why the Z bit is high or low following AND, OR, and EXCLUSIVE-OR. Briefly, the Z bit high says, "the result (accumulator) bit(s) is (are) equal to zero." The zero flag low says, "the result (accumulator) bit(s) is (are) high." Since this is somewhat counterintuitive, we should emphasize that when the accumulator has been cleared by a logical operation, then the zero flag will be set; if the accumulator has not been cleared, then the Z bit will be cleared. (As for the carry flag, we shall delay a theoretical discussion until the next chapter.)

When a logical COMPARE is performed between a mask and the accumulator, there occurs an arithmetic subtraction between the two registers (considering the mask as one of the registers); but the contents of the registers are restored following the COMPARE. Although we shall examine COMPARE in some detail in the next chapter, we can state the following rules for the C and Z flags following a COMPARE between data in a mask and data in the accumulator:

1. If the mask and the accumulator are equal, the zero flag is set.
2. If the mask is less than the accumulator, the carry flag is cleared.
3. If the mask is greater than the accumulator, the carry flag is set.

Direct Manipulation of the Carry Flag

The programmer will frequently wish to co-opt the carry flag to indicate the results of some computation to a calling routine by returning the C flag (either set or cleared) as a parameter to that calling routine. For example, suppose that a subroutine's function is to interrogate the control/status register of the peripheral storage device. If there are no error conditions pending, then the routine should report that condition back to the calling routine by returning the C flag clear; otherwise, the C flag will be returned set. The C flag (and only the C flag) can be directly manipulated (i.e., by a single instruction) in the following ways:

1. STC: sets the carry flag to 1, does not affect any registers
2. CMC: complements the carry flag (inverts its current value)
3. ORA   A: clears the carry flag, but leaves the accumulator intact.

Exercises

8-1. For a cardiac monitoring device, with a blinking light and an audible alarm, let us assume the following bit assignments in the CSR:

Function	Bit	Meaning
Activate alarm	0	1 = Activated
		0 = Silent
Activate monitor light	1	0 = Light off
		1 = Light on
Minimum pressure detect	2	0 = Blood pressure okay
		1 = Blood pressure at or below minimum
Error in device	7	0 = No error in system
		1 = Error in system

Define bit masks as symbols to be used in testing and manipulating the CSR bits.

8-2. Assume that IN 1 and OUT 1 are available to input and output the CSR to and from the accumulator. Use logical operations with the appropriate bit masks in order to accomplish the following (separate) tasks: (a) check for minimum cardiac pressure (call FLGERR if a low pressure condition exists); (b) check for system error in the hardware device (call FLGERR if a system error exists); (c) turn off the system-error detect bit; (d) activate the alarm; and (e) change state of light to opposite of current status.

8-3. Define a table called PLRNUM (player number) whose width is a single byte. This will be used in an automated scoring system. Allow for nine players on a team.

a. Write a verification routine (VERNUM) to search for the sequential position on the team of a player whose number is stored in WHOZIT, a single-byte memory location. At the end of the routine, the position of WHOZIT on the roster will be contained in the accumulator. If WHOZIT is not on the roster, then the accumulator will contain a −1. (Note: this is definitely a "housekeeping" routine.)

b. Now write the calling routine (CALLER) of VERNUM. It should place the player number form the accumulator into WHOZIT, then call VERNUM. Upon return from VERNUM, CALLER should query the results of the verification, using the carry flag as returned by VERNUM. CALLER should thereupon either set or clear bit 7 (summary error) in the CSR (which must be loaded into the accumulator). This updated CSR is then moved out to the CSR via the instruction OUT 1. In the case of a VERNUM error, CALLER in turn uses the carry bit to report an error condition to its calling program.

9

Manipulating Data: Arithmetic Operations

The 8080 instructions for arithmetic operations are easy to master, primarily because the only arithmetic operations permitted are adding, subtracting, incrementing, and decrementing. The factors which provide variety with the available instructions are (a) whether the data to be added or subtracted are immediate or not; (2) whether the carry bit is to be included in the addition/subtraction; and (3) whether the operation concerns a single byte or a register pair. For this discussion we shall group the instructions as follows: add/subtract (single byte), increment/decrement (single byte), add (register pair), increment/decrement (register pair), and convert accumulator to BCD (decimal adjust the accumulator)

Add/Subtract (Single Byte)

Once again the accumulator is the focus of activity. But this time *accumulator* really means what it says; it accumulates the sum or difference as calculated.

Add an Immediate Byte

There are two modes of addition, one that uses the carry bit in the computation, and one that does not.

1. Add the immediate-mode data to the contents of the accumulator. *Do not* use the carry bit in the computation: ADI *data.*
2. Add the immediate-mode data to the contents of the accumulator. *Include* the carry bit in the computation: ACI *data.*

Add a Nonimmediate Byte (from a Register or Memory)

As for the preceding immediate-data additions, we can either ignore or include the carry bit in the computation.

1. Ignore the carry bit in the addition: ADD *reg* (or M)
2. Include the carry bit in the addition: ADC *reg* (or M)

Subtract an Immediate Byte

The subtract operations are analogous to addition. However, *including the carry bit* in subtraction means "borrow from the carry bit".

1. Subtract this immediate data from the accumulator, ignoring the carry bit in the subtraction: SBI *data.*
2. Subtract this immediate data from the accumulator, including the carry bit in the subtraction: SCI *data.*

Subtract a Nonimmediate Byte (Register or Memory)

As in the preceding case of the additions, the two subtracts reference data either in single registers (A, B, C, D, E, H, L) or in memory, the byte in memory being referenced by the H,L pair.

1. Ignore the carry bit in the subtraction: SUB *reg* (or M)
2. Include the carry bit in the subtraction: SBC *reg* (or M)

Increment/Decrement (Single Byte)

Single Register

The two instructions are INR and DCR. These operations increment (or decrement) the specified register by one.

A Memory Location

Assuming that the H,L pair have been loaded with a proper memory address, we can increment or decrement the byte at that address by means of the instructions INR M or DCR M.

Add a Register Pair

This is the only instance in which the H,L pair is used as a true accumulator. The contents of the specified register pair are added to the H,L pair.

$$DAD \quad \begin{cases} B \\ D \\ H \\ SP \end{cases}$$

Increment/Decrement Register Pair

The two instructions are INX and DCX, and they serve to increment or decrement the specified register pair by 1.

$$\begin{Bmatrix} \text{INX} \\ \text{DCX} \end{Bmatrix} \quad \begin{Bmatrix} \text{B} \\ \text{D} \\ \text{H} \\ \text{SP} \end{Bmatrix}$$

Convert Accumulator to BCD

This instruction manipulates the accumulator only, and requires no operands:

    DAA   ;DECIMAL ADJUST THE ACCUMULATOR

The algorithm implemented by the hardware in performing the conversion is as follows. First, add 6 to the accumulator if (1) the auxiliary carry flag is high (as a result of a previous addition), or (2) the lower 4 bits of the accumulator are greater than 9. Then, add 6 to the upper half of the accumulator if (1) the carry flag is high (as a result of the previous addition instruction or as a result of the preceding algorithm, or (2) the upper 4 bits of the accumulator are greater than 9. Since this instruction is definitely for the type of operations that we have called "background" (and not normally part of real-time control functions), we refer the reader to the manufacturer's programming manual for further details.

Exercises

9-1. a. Add 15 and 14 (decimal), using immediate-mode data, and store the result in SUM. b. Add 15 to the quantity already stored in SUBTTL, and replace the new quantity in SUBTTL.

9-2. a. Subtract 34 from 171 (immediate mode). b. Subtract 3 from TKSLFT, leaving TKSLFT with the updated quantity.

9-3. a. Increment register B. b. Decrement the accumulator. c. Decrement TKSLFT (by 1). d. Increment the H,L pair.

9-4. a. Use DAD to add the double-byte quantity INTRVL to TTLTIM (both residing in memory locations). b. Compare TTLTIM with MAXTIM.

10 Control of Program Flow: Flags and Branching

A logic package (either software or hardware) that had no decision-making capability would be practically worthless, somewhat less flexible and hence less valuable than an electric lamp without a switch. The heart of the flexibility of electronic systems is the ability to execute or not execute predetermined sections of logic. In software this means the ability within a program to "jump" to another portion of the program, to "call" a routine whose logic can be shared by numerous sections of the code in the calling program, and to "return" from that routine to the point immediately following the "call."

Altering the flow of a program's execution is simple, as shall be seen in the case of the 8080 instructions that implement jump, call, and return. But there is a direct and very powerful effect on the readability of a program when these execution-altering instructions are inserted. This observation is only to serve as a warning to the programmer not to indulge in promiscuous branching within a program. In a later section we shall deal with programming style, in which branching is of utmost consideration. Indeed, we shall indicate how branching according to accepted standards can enhance the readability of programs.

The implementation of the three *unconditional* branching instructions are JMP, CALL, and RET (for "jump", "call", and "return," respectively). The format for each instruction is as follows:

1. JMP label: branch unconditionally to location specified by "label."
2. CALL routine: branch unconditionally to "routine." Upon encountering RET in "routine," execution will return automatically to instruction immediately following CALL.
3. RET: return to instruction in calling program immediately following CALL in calling program.

So much for the unconditional branches. Each of these branches (jump, call to routine, return from subroutine) may be executed conditionally, depending on the possible settings of the flag bits. For the conditional branch instructions, the first letters of the instructions are J, C, and R, respectively. The conditions, as specified in the remainder of the instructions, are encoded as follows:

1. -C, -NC: carry flag set, clear
2. -Z, -NZ: zero flag set, clear
3. -PE, -PO: parity even, odd
4. -P, -M: sign positive (plus), negative (minus)

85

Thus **JPE** means "jump if parity flag indicates even," **RNC** means "return from this subroutine if the carry bit is clear," **CP** means "call the subroutine indicated if the sign flag equals zero," and so on.

As we have indicated, for the purpose of comparing between bytes, the zero and carry flags will be the ones most frequently interrogated. And the manner of interrogation is in fact the set of conditions specified in Table 10-1. In the following section we shall present, in detail, how the typical instruction sequences involve the flags' settings in order to direct program execution.

Logical COMPARE and "Hidden" Subtraction

In order to utilize the full capabilities of the **CPI (CMP)** compare instruction for the 8080, it will be necessary to understand precisely what occurs during the subtraction of two numbers. Although on the surface a compare instruction appears to be simply a "logical" and not an "arithmetic" operation, the processor in fact performs a "hidden" subtract using the accumulator. Following the subtraction, the appropriate flags are set or cleared (carry and zero flags). Then the original contents of the accumulator are restored. The net result of a compare (either **CMP** or **CPI**) is that the carry and zero flags are set or cleared, depending on the results of the compare.

It is not the purpose of this text to provide a rigorous theoretical basis for binary arithmetic, subtraction in this case. However, we shall pause here long enough to supply the reader with an intuitive explanation of two's complement notation, plus some purely "crank-turning" methods for performing subtractions on paper. This should convince the reader that the setting and clearing of the flags by the 8080 indeed follows logically from the arithmetic process. Finally, we shall provide a reference summary chart to use in interpreting the zero and carry flags following a compare instruction. This summary, in turn, will give the reader a uniform means of implementing a structured programming style in our coding. The important secondary benefit from all this is that the reader will become totally familiar with all types of subtractions and the accompanying behavior of the flag bits.

The most fundamental issue for subtraction in particular is how the computer represents negative numbers. The answer is fairly straightforward: by two's complement notation for most systems. However, the justification for and the manipulation of two's complement numbers are somewhat less than transparent to most programmers. Therefore we shall offer first a discussion (not a proof) of representation of negative numbers by complement notation, appealing to everyday understanding of decimal numbers. Then we shall present a variety of conversion techniques.

Let us imagine a (very) hypothetical computer with the following unique characteristics: (1) the register (or word) length is a single decimal digit; and

Table 10-1
Examples of Two's Complement Arithmetic

Conversions:

Decimal	Binary	Hexadecimal
+25	0000 1001	19
−25	1110 0111	E7
+18	0001 0010	12
−18	1110 1110	EE

Worked Examples:[a]

Decimal	Binary (Subtrahend Unconverted)	Binary (Subtrahend Converted)		"Restored" Result	Decimal
(a) (25) − (18)	0001 1001 −0001 0010	0001 1001 +1110 1110 0000 0111	Carry: 0	+0000 0111	+07
(b) (18) − (25)	0001 0010 −0001 1001	0001 0010 +1110 0111 1111 1001	Carry: 1	−0000 0111	−07
(c) (+25) −(−18)	0001 1001 −1110 1110	0001 1001 +0001 0010 0010 1011	Carry: 1	+0010 1011	+43
(d) (−25) −(+18)	1110 0111 −0001 0010	1110 0111 +1110 1110 1101 0101	Carry: 0	−0010 1011	−43
(e) (−25) −(−18)	1110 0111 −1110 1110	1110 0111 +0001 0010 1111 1001	Carry: 1	−0000 0111	−07

Table 10-1. *(Continued)*

	Decimal	Binary (Subtrahend Unconverted)		Binary (Subtrahend Converted)	"Restored" Result	Decimal
(f)	(+18)	0001 0010		0001 0010		
	−(−25)	−1110 0111		+0001 1001		
			Carry: 1	0010 1011	+0010 1011	+43
(g)	(−18)	1110 1110		1110 1110		
	−(+25)	−0001 1001		+1110 0111		
			Carry: 0	1101 0101	−0010 1011	−43
(h)	(−18)	1110 1110		1110 1110		
	−(−25)	−1110 0111		+0001 1001		
			Carry: 0	0000 0111	+0000 0111	+07

Note: The carry flag is automatically complemented following a subtraction.

[a]The flag is used to determine the sign for the "restored" result in these examples. But when the two original values have different signs, then the carry bit should be reinverted to produce the proper sign of the restored result.

(2) the hardware implementation for representing that single digit is a 10-state flip-flop that can assume values from 0 to 9; and (3) only additions (and not subtractions) are possible in the hardware. (As for the 10-state flip-flop, semantic purists may prefer a totally different name for this apparatus, perhaps "flip-flap-floop- . . . -flop" or "flip-flop $\times$ 5" to indicate the 10 possible states.) Suppose that we are to perform a single-digit subtraction on this machine, 9 − 6 for instance. Algebraically, this would be equivalent to 9 + (−6). This is fortunate, inasmuch as the machine cannot perform subtraction anyway. The only trick now is to make that −6 into something that can be added properly by the machine and yet provide the correct answer. The "trick" we shall use is to subtract the absolute value (6) from 10 and consider the result of that subtraction as the term to be added to the 9. We call this particular form the *ten's complement*. (Never mind for the moment how that subtraction is possible nor where the 10 comes from.) The new expression, ready now for the machine to add, is 9 + 4. As every schoolboy/girl knows, the answer is 13. But not every schoolboy/girl is limited to a single digit for the length of numbers. Our machine, since it is only a single digit wide, recognizes only the 3 as the answer, with the 1 as something that gets "rippled out." By the way, 3 is the correct answer to the problem.

But we should not leave the reader in suspense regarding the 10 and the preceding sleight-of-hand subtraction. So now for their explanation. The rule (somewhat formal) for obtaining the correct number to subtract from (called the *minuend*) is as follows.

Calculation of minuend. Raise the base of the numbering system to the power equal to the number of digits allowable in a memory location (= the word length of the machine). In the example, the base is 10 and the word length is 1, so the minuend is $10^1 = 10$.

We shall generalize this to more realistic machines in a moment. As for the "hidden" subtraction, we must unfortunately delay this matter until we discuss binary numbers, since for binary numbers the conversion to two's complement notation is trivial and can be totally mechanical and not arithmetic at all (for which the machine is grateful).

Let us now upgrade the hardware to a two-digit word model, still with 10-state flip-flops for each digit. This time the problem is to subtract 7 from 25. The first step is to decide on the proper minuend for the conversion to ten's complement. Since the word length is now two digits, the minuend is $10^2 = 100$. So the ten's complement of 7 is 100 − 7 = 93. Next we add 25 + 93 = 118. Of course, in the machine, only the two rightmost digits are useful in the calculation, and 18 is indeed the answer expected.

By now the reader should be asking how the computer remembers that the 93 in the problem was really a ten's complement representation of 7 and not really the positive value 93. One way might be for the system to set some sign flag to tell the world that this is really the representation of a negative number. Another method (the one actually used by most machines) is to dedicate the most significant digit of the word to the task of representing the sign of the number. Thus the 9 in 93 tells us that this is really a negative number in ten's complement notation. (A zero in the most significant position of the word indicates a positive number, not in ten's complement form.) In the case of a decimal machine, such as this one, this seems outlandishly wasteful of information, since we are throwing away eight other states of the most significant digit (1 through 8) once we indicate the sign of the number. In a binary (and not a decimal) machine, as luck would have it, a single binary digit is exactly appropriate to such a task. The highest-order digit is used to indicate the sign of the number, and no states of the digit are "thrown away," since there are only two states of a binary digit.

Before leaving the binary machine, let us expand the word length to 16. This time the problem is to subtract 350 from 500. The "magic minuend" we need for converting to ten's complement for a 16-digit decimal machine is 10^{16} = 10,000,000,000,000,000. This number minus 350 = 9,999,999,999,999,650. The original problem, with the number to be subtracted (the *subtrahend*) now translated into ten's complement notation, is as follows:

$$\begin{array}{ll} 0\ 000\ 000\ 000\ 000\ 500 & (+500) \\ \underline{+\ \ 9\ 999\ 999\ 999\ 999\ 650} & \underline{(-350)} \\ 10\ 000\ 000\ 000\ 000\ 150 & (+150) \end{array}$$

Note that the leftmost 1 has been "rippled" out the end of the register, leaving only the correct answer to the problem in the register itself. The 0 in position 15 (16th digit from the right) indicates that the answer is positive.

Let us now leave behind this mythical realm of 10-state flip-flops. If the reader by now has a more firm grasp of how n's complement notation functions in subtraction, then the excursus has been well worthwhile. It is time now to look at the real world of two-state flip-flops, i.e., the binary computer. For the conversion of binary numbers to express "negative," the term used is "two's complement." And the algorithm is precisely the same as for the preceding decimal examples. Let us assume from the outset that the register width (as well as the width of each addressable memory location) is 8 bits, as indeed is true in the 8080. Our "magic minuend" now is 2^8 = 256_{10} = $1\ 0000\ 0000_2$. The first subtraction problem is:

$$29_{10} - 17_{10} \text{ or } \qquad 1D_{16} - 11_{16}$$

1. Convert 11_{16} to two's complement:

$$\begin{array}{ll} 1\ 0000\ 0000 & (2^8) \\ -\ \ 0001\ 0001 & (11_{16}) \\ \hline \quad\ 1110\ 1111 & (EF_{16} = 239_{10}) \end{array}$$

2. Perform addition with two's complement:

$$\begin{array}{ll} \quad\ 0001\ 1101 & (1D) \\ +\ \ 1110\ 1111 & (EF) \\ \hline 1\ 0000\ 1100 & (0C = 12_{10}) \end{array}$$

Note that 12 is the correct answer and that the sign bit equals 0, all of which is proper. Anyone with previous practice in hand calculations with binary arithmetic should be able to do the preceding subtraction and conversion with no great difficulty. Let us denote this whole method of conversion to two's complement as "purely arithmetic," since it involves outright subtraction with borrowing in the traditional sense. Such a method is not only tedious when performed by hand, but it is also impossible in most computer architectures. (Recall too that the original purpose of conversion to two's complement was to avoid subtraction altogether.)

A second method of performing this subtraction for conversion to two's complement we shall call "purely algorithmic" (for want of a better term). Ther are two very simple steps to the algorithm: (1) complement each bit of the number to be converted, and (2) add 1 to the result of step 1. In the case of 17_{10} ($= 11_{16}$), we would proceed as follows:

1. Complement the original number:

0001 0001	Original number
1110 1110	Complemented form

2. Add 1 to the result of step 1:

$$\begin{array}{l} 1110\ 1110 \\ 0000\ 0001 \\ \hline 1110\ 1111 \qquad \text{The correct two's complement} \end{array}$$

The third method of converting to two's complement we shall call "purely mechanical," only because there is even less arithmetic involved than in the previous method. This strategy involves a right-to-left scan-and-complement algorithm which may be stated as follows: (1) moving from right to left across the binary number, find the first 1 in the number, and (2) beginning with the next digit to the left of the 1 encountered in step 1, complement all the remaining bits in the number. Applying this process to the number 0001 0001, we proceed as follows (C here means "complement", N means "not complement"):

```
0001  0001
CCCC  CCCN
1110  1111      Correct complement
```

All this attention to a process which the computer does in a very transparent manner (in the case of outright subtractions via SUB or SBB in the 8080) may seem to be a waste of time. And it may seem even more so in the case of logical compares, in which the subtractions are not only transparent but almost totally hidden. Recall that we said that in a compare (CMP or CPI), the contents of the accumulator are restored to their status prior to the compare instruction. But what is the status of the carry and zero flags? We must now close in on the important information borne by these flags following logical compare instructions.

A compare is really a "nondestructive" subtraction. That is, a byte located either in an immediate location within the instruction, in a register, or in a memory location is subtracted from the contents of the accumulator. The two flags are set accordingly, and the contents of the accumulator are then immediately restored by the processor. Let us look at the zero and carry flags.

The function and interpretation of the zero flag is intuitively simple. It is set (turned on) when the result of the nondestructive subtraction from the accumulator produces a zero result. In terms of a logical compare, this means clearly that the 2 bytes being compared were exactly equal. When the zero flag is clear (turned off) following a compare, then we know that the 2 bytes were not equal.

The operation and interpretation of the carry flag is not so intuitively clear, but we are now prepared to convince ourselves of why it behaves the way the manual says it behaves, thanks to our familiarity with binary subtraction. Remember that "extra" high-order 1 that got "rippled out" of the register during the hand calculations? That single bit did not simply "fall on the floor" as it was shifted left. Instead, during a subtraction (either explicitly arithmetic, as described in Chapter 9, or "hidden") the resulting carry bit is complemented. The final state of the carry flag following a subtraction is therefore the complement of whatever one might expect from the computation. All this makes the subtraction process somewhat more complicated than one might follow easily by mere intuition every time one wishes to perform a logical compare. Therefore, the reader should study carefully the worked example in Table 10-1. Once convinced of how the "hidden subtraction" operates, the reader can rely upon the summary table offered later in this chapter.

Having followed the mechanics through all the possible permutations of subtraction involving two signed numbers, we are (finally) prepared to summarize the behavior of the carry bit (carry flag) in the 8080. Let us call the first number (minuend) A, as in *accumulator;* we shall use B for the second number (subtrahend). When the *signs* of A and B are the *same,* then

CARRY = 0 when $A \geqslant B$
CARRY = 1 when $A < B$

When the signs of A and B are *opposite,* then

CARRY = 1 when $A > B$
CARRY = 0 when $A < B$

("Greater than" and "less than" here mean signed, relational value, not absolute value of the numbers.)

The preceding summary can be checked very quickly by referring to the 10 examples in Table 10-1. Simply note the signs of the numbers in the original decimal expressions and the relative values of A and B, then note the value of the carry bit.

As a summary of both the carry and zero flags in compares, we offer the summary chart in Table 10-2.

Table 10-2
CARRY and ZERO Flags Following COMPARE (CMP) of Accumulator with Register or Memory

	A:*reg*/M	CARRY	ZERO
Signs same:	=	0	1
	>	0	0
	<	1	0
Signs opposite:	>	1	0
	<	0	0

Exercises

The point of this chapter is to derive Table 10-2 as "honestly" as possible, not to teach two's complement arithmetic per se. However, since subtraction involves two's complement so frequently, it would be good to check ourselves by converting a few quantities. In each case, give the binary first, then the hexadecimal of the two's complement of each of the numbers.

10-1. 22 (decimal)

10-2. 19H

10-3. 63Q

10-4. 0100 1110B

10-5. 0FFH

11 Top-Down Design and Programming Style

This chapter is written with a particular type of reader in mind. The typical learner of a new computer system is intensely interested in mastering the instruction set of that computer's language (the assembler language of the 8080 in this case). And it is also quite likely that the reader of this particular text, because it is written about a computer that typically is used to "make things go," will be more satisfied personally if indeed he can make his "thing" go. Such a designer/programmer often views the language of the computer, with all its rules and restrictions, as a necessary evil to be endured until the job is done (the "thing" is running under the computer's control and finally in production and shipped to the customers). For such a reader the suggestion to incorporate some sort of style into the coding is outrageous, an extravagant demand.

The problem here is not that designers, whether hardware or software, are untidy souls. It demands an immense degree of clarity to get a program to run, and any programmer would agree that code should be "clear," "tidy," and "presentable." The real problem lies with the semantics of the term *style*. In natural language, as language is used by writers, particularly artistic writers, *style* refers to the manner in which an author utilizes the basic building blocks of the writing craft to achieve the final product. It normally refers to written expression that is "artistic" or "poetic," perhaps even poetry itself. And if it is true that artists and poets are not made, then few of us indeed could hope to aspire to a mastery of style—in that narrow but highly popular sense of the word. So it is little wonder that an engineer, pressed by the cold realities of design and production schedules, should be somewhat less than enthusiastic over the issue of style in programming; it is a frill that simply must be ignored in the interests of getting the job done.

But we can learn a valuable lesson from *style*, as the word is more fully defined for natural language. Faulkner, Hemingway, Frost, and Elliot indeed use styles by which to personalize their works. But hundreds of journalists, technical writers, and other expository authors impose a style on their writing for a quite different purpose—*clarity*. The main distinction between *styles* in the creative sense and *styles* in the expository sense is that the rules of the former are personal, internal, and normally not evident to the reader without careful analysis; the various rules of style for expository writing, on the other hand, are more easily described and shared by the entire community of expository writers. Here it is as though the expository author subordinates his individuality to the rules of the

95

game, the object of the game being to communicate ideas as free of ambiguity as possible.

If we think of "programming style" in the nonartistic sense of *style*, then we can claim that a programmer should subordinate his freedom and individuality to some given rules of coding, the object of this exercise being to communicate the code to others as effortlessly and unambiguously as possible. The sad reality of programming practice, as it continues (in spite of major innovations announced and described 10 years ago), is that programmers still care very much about developing and debugging code (getting it to run); they refuse to be concerned about how their code is to be modified and maintained (kept running).

And just how significant is the issue of maintenance? The average programmer's secret wish is that his code will have been designed and written so cleverly that it will apply to all possible environments and will never need modification. The hard economic truth of software budgeting is that well over half the industrial software dollars go for maintenance. Within the average computer science curriculum, the problem of a program's maintenance is nonexistent; a programming project is completed, and a course credit is earned. Occasionally, student "slave labor" may be used in the maintenance activities of a university's operating system or other software support activities, but this only obscures the harsh reality that total software engineering costs in industry range from $25,000 to $40,000 per man-year ($11.09 to $17.73 per hour). So whether the code in question is for an accounts receivable system or for a microprocessor-controlled pressure monitoring system, the issue of programming style is in no way an extravagance but an utter economic necessity.

If the reader has looked ahead in this chapter (as a reader always should), he or she has recognized that the bulk of this and the next chapters have to do with structured programming. The reader may therefore have guessed that the author is now to suggest that structured programming is the way to set the software world right. The reader is only one-third right. The path toward software production that is economically viable in the long-term sense is threefold:

1. *Realize that every program written will have to be modified.* This is not meant to encourage sloppy design or coding techniques ("It'll be redone anyway, so I'll just throw something together for the first time around"). On the contrary, a designer/programmer should realize that a piece of original code may never be totally scrapped (although it may be an act of mercy to do so). The main skeletal structure of that program will be used and reused for as many "generations" of applications as possible. The original design must therefore take into account all the foreseeable modifications that will be made to the program: whole new routines, hardware and system configurations, user interface modifications, etc. And, if this is desirable for software in general, it is imperative for real-time, hardware interface applications in particular. First, the presence of a specially designed hardware package that "converses" with real-time software introduces a large number of unknowns into the total system. In other words,

it is mathematically impossible to write "correct" software for real-time applications on the first go-around. Second, real-time software must make provisions for "tweaking" (or fine-tuning), a standard procedure in hardware design. Typically, "tweaking" will occur in timing and delay loops of the software as the characteristics of the hardware and of the total system become better defined.

2. *Realize that someone else will modify the code.* There is absolutely no exception to this rule. Modification can occur only in one of two ways: (1) a person other than the original coder must modify the existing code (which he or she must read and understand thoroughly); (2) the original author must modify the existing code. But in the second case, that author is now "someone else." Only a genius capable of multiple simultaneous chess competition at the master's level could hope to retain all the intricacy of his own computer code written months or even weeks before. It is embarrassing and wasteful to have to relearn one's own code every six weeks if that code is not written expressly to be maintained.

3. *Write the code in a standard structured format.* The first two rules were largely psychological; this one is strictly procedural. (The readers who already have had experience in structured programming may skip to the beginning of the next chapter after finishing this paragraph.) Hardware designers have long recognized that circuit diagrams are largely self-documenting. Fortunately (for hardware documentation), only a very few of the possible hardware logic functions are used in actual designs. This restriction guarantees that a given circuit will be more readable and hence easier to modify than would otherwise be possible. In a similar spirit, structured programming offers the possibility of software that is readable by the entire programming community and by interested hardware designers. There is a tradeoff, of course. The software designer must impose re-restrictions on the program, restrictions that reach all the way "up" to the initial specification of the program.

In the remainder of this chapter, we shall survey briefly the mechanics of structured programming (it is *not* simply coding without GO TO's). Then we shall offer some rather convincing arguments why top-down structured programming is the most painless, cost-effective, and theoretically "nice" way to generate code. We shall begin the next chapter by implementing structured code purely in assembly language for the 8080.

By now there are very few programmers (professional or student) who have not heard of structured programming and so not have at least a vague notion of its characteristics. Nearly every keynote address at every conference dealing with software pleads with the programming community to use it, and it has become *the* established state-of-the-art strategy for design and encoding. To the phrase *structured programming* we shall add *top-down* so that we shall consider *top-down structured programming* to be defined as follows.

Top-down structured programming: a definition. A method for solving a given problem or implementing a given definition, in which the problem or definition is more specifically refined at each step of the procedure until a final step of refinement results in executable code. The same limited set of syntactic structures is used at every stage of the problem's refinement.

Before attempting even to paraphrase this rather formal definition, let us implement a simple but not hypothetical product, a pressure monitoring device. (It could be for cabin air pressure in aircraft, for pressure *differential* between the surfaces of an airplane wing, for water pressure in deep-sea diving, or for osmotic pressure in kidneys, depending on the hardware with which the microprocessor is to be interfaced.) The first (topmost) level of the definition might be as follows.

Functional description. As long as the pressure being monitored by the device is satisfactory (i.e., above or below a given threshold, depending on the application), a green light will turn on for one-half second then turn off for another one-half second. (This continuous on-off cycle is to assure the user that the processor is still in operation.) Whenever the pressure moves to an unsatisfactory level (i.e., crosses the threshold), a red light (instead of the green light) will repeat on and off in half-second intervals. The "on" portion of the red light cycle will be accompanied by an audible "beep." The audio signal will therefore also be on a one-second repeating cycle for as long as the pressure is unsatisfactory.

As a description of a product, the preceding "definition" is quite clear, so clear that the typical programmer is liable to begin immediately to flowchart and then to write code based on that description and based on the flowchart. (Or worse, coding may begin without anything except the prose description.) The good news is that such a description, accompanying flowchart (or other such logic aid), and associated code can be implemented quickly and may even work. The bad news is that the resulting code will inevitably have a structure that is ancestrally bound to the flowchart, which in turn was "generated" by the original description. That description itself was structured in a manner totally unique to the particular problem. And thus in two brief paragraphs we have documented an all too typical "garden path" that has led to thousands (millions, perhaps) of programs in existence, each of whose structures uniquely reflect the application for which they were written and which are therefore difficult or impossible to read. Most important, they are difficult to extend to other applications since they probably will have been implemented in a nongeneral, inflexible manner. It should now be clear that what is needed is some sort of formal, uniform discipline that can be exerted on the definition of a problem *at its highest level.* In this way, the resulting code could indeed implement the solution to the problem, but that code's structure would be immediately recognizable and the code therefore readable (and maintainable) by programmers at large. We are deliberately halting the development of the PMD-V1

(Pressure Monitoring Device, Version 1) for the moment until we acquire the necessary design tools.

We shall now decree that henceforth the following and only the following structural devices shall be available to us in defining a problem at any level of refinement (including the topmost "description" level):

1. *Sequential execution.* "Do *x*, then *y*, then *z*."
2. *Selection based on test.* "If *a* (is true), then do *x*, else (otherwise) do *y*."
3. *Conditional iteration.* "Do *x*, and keep on doing *x* as long as (while) *a* is true."

The "structuring mechanisms" can be depicted and described more tersely as in Figure 11-1. A *top-down structured program* can now be defined in a very casual way to be a program that utilizes only the three basic mechanisms depicted in Figure 11-1 and that continues from its topmost definitional level

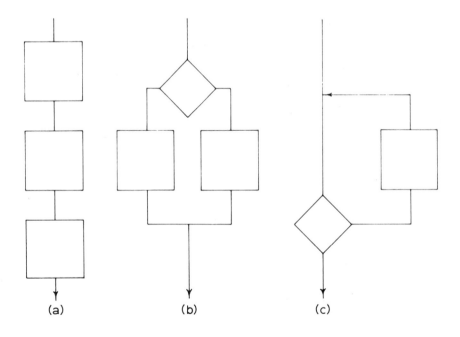

(a)   (b)   (c)

Figure 11-1. Basic Components of Structured Programming: (a) Sequential Execution, (b) Selection Based on Test (IF . . . THEN . . . ELSE), and (c) Conditional Iteration (WHILE . . . DO).

"downward," all the way to actual computer code, using only those mechanisms. (A more technical description of this topmost-to-bottommost progression is "stepwise refinement.")

Before leaving these three "building-block" flowcharts, let us emphasize heavily what may appear so trivial as to go unnoticed. In all three of the flowcharts there is only a single entry point and a single exit. This is not accidental. It provides a hefty "handle" on the problem of correctness-proving. Given single-entry/single-exit structures, it then becomes feasible to devise rigorous methods for guaranteeing the correctness of whole programs, as they are being designed. In practical terms this means that in designing a module (whether at the actual coding level or not), we can accurately specify the input(s) to and the output(s) from the module. And when the code is actually written, we can easily test these hypotheses to prove the correctness of the module. And most important from the standpoint of modifiability, one can always be certain that the bottommost line of code in a module is also the only exit point of the module. One can therefore be much more certain that added or deleted code will allow the program still to function properly. We shall take up the actual implementation of structured code for the 8080 as we enter the coding stage of the various design exercises.

For now, let us return to the task of redefinition of the PMD-V1. (If you suspect that management may be overly threatened by the term *redefinition*, then call it a "scheduled design review.") Keeping the three "building blocks" well in mind, see if you can spot them in the rather wordy description handed you by the project coordinator. *As long as* sounds like a WHILE. And as we read the entire description, we sense a very large IF ... THEN ... ELSE looming over the entire scene: "If the pressure's OK, then flash the green light on and off, but if it's not, then flash the red light and sound the beeper." And what about that flashing and beeping? There appears to be a constant time-keeping function at work here. Following the decision about the pressure, the appropriate light (and perhaps the beeper) is activated. There's a delay of one-half second. The signal(s) are shut off. Finally, another half-second delay occurs before the decision is to be made again regarding the pressure level. A simple case of *sequential execution.*

1. Delay for one-half second.
2. Test pressure and select appropriate light (and perhaps audio signal).
3. Turn on appropriate signal(s), as selected in step 2.
4. Delay for one-half second.
5. Turn off signal(s).

So a simple sequence of five processes takes us through a single cycle of operation of the device. All that we need now to keep the device going nonstop is to specify that steps 1 through 5 of the sequential execution be repeated indefinitely. *Repeat indefinitely* is not exactly among our "bag of tricks" (we have only three such tricks), so we must make do with what we have. Which of the three "structuring mechanisms" handles looping of this type? (Hint: DO-WHILE.) All we need to do is to specify some condition that we know will be true forever so that the DO of the DO-WHILE is actually a DO-FOREVER.

We are now ready for a more truly structured definition of the operation of the PMD-V1, based solely on the three structuring mechanisms we have limited ourselves to as universally understood elements of our design vocabulary.

Structured Narrative of PMD-V1
Execute indefinitely
   Turn off signals
   Test the pressure
   If the pressure is satisfactory,
   Then
      Select "green" for visual
      Select "silent" for audio
   Else
      Select "red" for visual
      Select "beep" for audio
   End (of IF ... THEN ... ELSE block)
   Activate proper visual and audio signals
   Do a half-second delay
End (of "execute indefinitely" block)

The reader who has a distaste for flowcharting (in the traditional sense) will be pleased to note that we have "defined" the product without the need of a flowchart. (Indeed many proponents of structured programming argue that the trivial number of sequencing mechanisms in turn renders flowcharting a trivial exercise; in this sense, a structured program truly could be said to be self-documenting.) But just to convince ourselves that we have played by the rules, let us flowchart the operation of the PMV-V1, as in Figure 11-2.

The programmer who is not at home with a top-down strategy probably is feeling uneasy at this point over "code" that is really no code at all, just a natural language (English) paraphrase of the problem that happens to conform to rules of structured programming. Any runable code at this point appears to be just a fiction, something that is only suggested by the English paraphrase. All this is true. In fact, the nature of top-down design is such that the present level of description always assumes an "imaginary" implementation at the next level down. For example, *turn off the signals* describes perfectly what we wish to accomplish, but that phrase by itself would be meaningless to the computer. As we shall see shortly, another level "down" in the implementation will specify precisely the hardware register to be accessed and the particular bit mask configuration that actually will turn off both devices. The point is that the designer/programmer must learn to live with unreal specifications which may remain

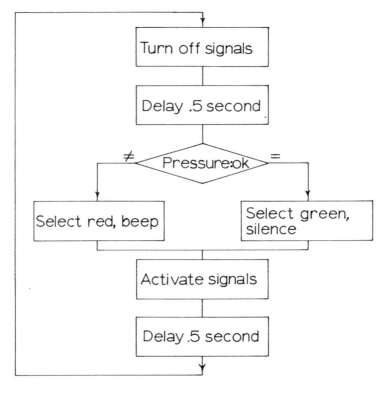

Figure 11-2. Flowchart of Pressure Monitoring Device

unreal at each step downward until the final, lowest level of the implementation, that of the computer code itself.

But as any programmer knows, even executable computer code can contain levels of reality; we see this all the time in programs that use calls to subroutines. Let us see how the PMV-V1 may be specified with actual 8080 assembler code at the very next level down from the English description. (We have skipped an entire step in the process, that of pseudo-code, only to demonstrate that even an imaginary program can be executable.)

```
LOOP1:   CALL SIGOFF       ;TURN OFF SIGNALS
         CALL TSTPRS       ;TEST PRESSURE, SELECT SIGNALS
         CALL SIGON        ;ACTIVATE SIGNALS
         CALL DELAY        ;WAIT ONE-HALF SECOND
         JMP LOOP1         ;KEEP LOOPING FOREVER
```

The program at this level is now executable, provided that each of the sub-routines in turn exist as executable code. At this early stage of implementation the subroutines may consist only of a single line each: RET (return from sub-routine). Their only function at this stage would be to return execution im-mediately to the main loop. The entire second level of the program (the level of code called directly by the main loop) would be:

```
SIGOFF:    RET
TSTPRS:    RET
SIGON:     RET
DELAY:     RET
```

We call these subroutines *stubs;* they are simply dummy routines that serve only to keep the calling sequence moving along properly.

We now have a design (and even some actual code, albeit premature) that is said to be modular. Every portion of the program is totally isolated one from the other. (Admittedly, this sort of extreme would probably be unnecessary in a program of our size.) It obviously costs execution time to issue calls to and from subroutines, when all the logic *could* be implemented "in-line" within LOOP1 itself. Why then invest in the overhead of modularization?

The most obvious benefit from the tradeoff is readability. When someone other than the programmer picks up code for the PMD-V1, he can easily "get the big picture" by reading only LOOP1. He does not have to wade through the detailed code concerning device registers, timing delays, decisions about red and green lights, all of which are implemented within lower-level code. If he is interested in the details of any portion of the total program, he can turn im-mediately to that module of the program and read the details of that module alone.

But modularity has some payoffs that are even more practical. In programs of considerable size, in which several programmers may participate, it is a simple matter for each programmer to write his own module of code, test that module by itself (using a dummy calling routine), and then "plug" the new module into the real program in place of the original stub. In this way pro-grammers are not all accessing and writing into the same sequence of statements as they contribute their parts.

Modularity also has some value if the product undergoes redefinition, either before it is released or even after it has been in the field for awhile. For example, suppose the external stimuli of lights and beepers on a device get changed to, say, a wailing siren or a printed report on a CRT screen.

It may happen that a particular program that has been running satisfactorily on one particular processor may be needed for execution on a totally different machine. It is inevitable that the original program will have to be rewritten for the new processor. But it is very likely that the original structure of the program can be preserved intact during the rewriting process; redesign time is therefore kept to an absolute minimum. The English narrative and the pseudo-code steps would not have to be altered, and it is likely that the main, calling loop might even run intact on some machine other than the 8080.

Real-time applications provide the strongest of all motivations for modularized programs. Particularly during debugging and hardware integration (the checkout phase during which the processor is finally tested with the real hardware it was planned to drive, control, or monitor), it frequently happens that a programmer cannot be sure whether some bug is due to his own code, to some mistaken assumption between hardware and software, or to some catastrophic hardware failure in a chip or on a printed circuit board. At such a time it is very convenient to bypass the hardware-associated logic of the code completely in order to be sure that the software logic is still functioning properly (or at least as it was designed to function). When all the hardware-associated logic has been isolated from the outset into modules, such a temporary bypass becomes a very simple matter. Or, instead of a total bypass, the programmer may wish to insert some sort of software simulator in place of the hardware module(s), some routine(s) that will generate some signal to assure the designer(s) that the routine is indeed getting executed, that the parameters passed to the routine are indeed correct, and that proper parameters returned from the routine permit the total program to keep functioning. This sort of simulation or total bypass would be virtually impossible unless the program had been designed in modules from the outset.

But now it is time for the "real" thing. Let us take the subroutines one by one and see how the software will do the actual monitoring and controlling. This we shall do by means of a pseudo-code which could next be translated into actual computer code. But before we write any code at all, we must specify the necessary hardware interface structures that are available to us. (The whole issue of interface structures was discussed in Chapter 3.)

Normally the hardware designers will have decided on the bit assignments in the necessary control/status registers before the programmer designs his code. In top-down software design, even these necessary details can be left open until the very last step. Let us suppose that for the PMD-V1 there is a single control/status register in memory location 1000. The register is a single byte (8 bits) in length, and the various bits are assigned as follows:

Bit Number	Setting	Meaning
0	0	Pressure at or above threshold
	1	Pressure below threshold
1	0	Pressure at or below threshold
	1	Pressure above threshold

Bit Number	Setting	Meaning
2	0	Green light off
	1	Green light on
3	0	Red light off
	1	Red light on
4	0	Audio signal silent
	1	Audio signal sounding
5-7	Unused	

Note that bits 0 and 1 are read by the program and are therefore *status* bits; bits 2 through 4 will be written to by the software and are therefore *control* bits. Recall that the PMD-V1 will be used to monitor pressures, either to warn of low (below a threshold) or high (above a threshold). Therefore, depending on the particular application, either bit 0 or bit 1 will be tested for a possible too-high/too-low pressure condition. Furthermore, it will be possible to test for the condition of the pressure's being precisely at the threshold by testing for both bits 0 and 1 to be low (off). In future versions of the PMD we would like for both the red and the green lights to go on when the pressure is exactly at the threshold as set in the hardware. This will allow for greater precision when adjusting the threshold setting to a known pressure. So although a single bit in the CSR may have sufficed to tell us whether pressure is too high or too low, we shall use two bits for the projected enhancements of the product.

We should note finally that bits 0 and 1 are written to by the hardware and that bits 2 through 4 are read by the hardware. *Read* in this case means that whenever any of bits 2 through 4 are set high by the software, then the associated light(s) and/or audio signals are turned on in the hardware.

106

Exercises

11-1. Draw a flowchart for the FOR I = . . . type of loop, as seen in FORTRAN and BASIC. Which of the three structured programming sequencing mechanisms does the chart resemble? How could a FOR loop be implemented, using only these three mechanisms? Show two options for the location of the test on I, and state the implication of each operation.

11-2. Some programmers argue that "bit-banging" is best done in assembler. But let us write a pseudo-code routine (structured, of course) that accomplishes the following: (a) decrements TIMLFT, (b) tests for a zero value in TIMLFT, (c) if zero, then sets TIMOUT bit in CSR, (d) if nonzero, then clears TIMOUT bit in CSR and calls DOAGIN, and (e) repeats this all over again, until time-out occurs. Remember, the code should utilize only the three basic structuring mechanisms of structured programming.

12

Implementing Control Structures in the 8080 Assembler

In Chapter 11 we introduced and discussed briefly the three control structures that are necessary (the *only* necessary mechanisms) in a program that is truly structured. And we have indicated at some length the behavior of the carry and zero flags in connection with the following operations in particular:

1. AND: isolates bits(s) in the accumulator, then sets or clears the zero flag to indicate zero or nonzero result in the accumulator.
2. DECREMENT: decrements the contents of a byte, then sets or clears the zero flag, as above.
3. COMPARE: performs a "hidden" subtraction (using accumulator as the subtrahend), then leaves carry and zero flags set or cleared to indicate all possible equality and inequality relationships between the items being compared.

We noted that the states of these flags in turn are used to govern branching within the program. Although it is popularly said that the essence of structured programming is the elimination of the GO TO, it is also recognized that to implement structured programming style strictly in assembly language *necessitates* branching—much branching. But the condition that we shall lay on branching in this chapter is that branching (jumps) must be done solely to implement the control structures of structured programming. This chapter, therefore, will demonstrate how to express the prime control structures in the idiom of the 8080 assembler. Since conditional branching is a key ingredient to these structures, we shall devote considerable attention, first at a pseudo-language level, to a proper translation of the flowcharts studied in the previous chapter. Then we shall translate that pseudo-code into actual 8080 code, relying totally on the facility gained in the use of the carry and zero flags. It is expected that the techniques presented here will not be viewed simply as yet another "bag of tricks" for clever programmers, but that the control structures presented will constitute an easily mastered and powerful set of "primitives" from which any and all programs can be constructed. (As for tricky programming, that is a commodity of which far less, not more, is needed. The strategy we are about to present is possibly the most "unclever" approach to programming to be found today.)

Recall that there are three and only three primary control structures necessary in structured programming. (Theorists may argue strongly for additional "primary" structures, but these three can be proven to be the "most primary.") Recall that the control structures are (1) *sequential execution* (execute code A, then execute code B, then. . . .); (2) *selection based on test* (if condition true, then execute code A, else execute code B); and (3) *conditional iteration* (execute code A while condition true). (Note that the paraphrase given for each preceding structure is only representative.) Study again the primary structures, together with their associated flowcharts (in Figure 11-1), as they were presented in the previous chapter.

Sequential Execution

The flowchart for sequential execution looks so trivial that it hardly seems worthwhile to comment on its significance in structured programming. Consider the following two sequences of 8080 code (noting only line A and B of each block):

```
SAMPL1:
        LDX      H,COUNTR      ; SET H,L→VALUE FOR
                               ; COUNTER
        MOV      B,M           ; INITIALIZE B AS COUNTER
        MVI      A,03FH        ; (A)
LOOP1:
        ADI      A,05          ; (B)
        DCR      B             ; ONE LESS TRIP THROUGH
                               ; LOOP
        JNZ      LOOP1         ;

SAMPL2:
        LDX      H,COUNTR      ;
        MOV      B,M           ;
        MVI      A,03FH        ; (A)
LOOP2:
        CALL     SUBR          ; (B)
        DCR      B             ;
        JNZ      LOOP2
```

The major structural difference between these two sequences is that the second one contains a jump to a subroutine SUBR. Now suppose that within SUBR the programmer had implemented a few DO-WHILE's and IF . . . THEN . . . ELSE's. Or, suppose that SUBR were a routine filled with unreadable, convoluted, unstructured logic. Would SAMPL2 still be considered a case of strict sequential execution? The answer is an unqualified yes. Recall that the nature of stepwise refinement is such that we view a system in successively lower levels of refinement until finally reaching the actual computer instructions. When we branch to SUBR, we do it unconditionally. That is the first criterion that makes SAMPL2 a legitimate example of sequential execution. Furthermore, as we view SUBR strictly from the perspective (level) of SAMPL2, it is as though we (rather blindly) put SUBR into a black box, ignoring for the moment any of the logical details of SUBR whatsoever. In fact, SUBR may not be structured at all. It may be an exceedingly sloppy routine, difficult to read and to modify, but one that can be left alone within its box because it works. In the larger context of the entire system, therefore, SUBR is equivalent in structure to a single computer instruction when viewed solely as a routine executed unconditionally between the instruction just prior to its call and the instruction just following the return to the calling program.

Selection Based on Test (IF . . . THEN . . . ELSE)

We shall mention at this point that many of the comments and warnings relative to selection based on test apply equally to conditional iteration, inasmuch as both types of structures utilize a decision box in their logical flow.

In the discussion of structured programming thus far we have said little about the relative difficulty of implementing the primary structures in assembly language (as compared to a high-level language designed primarily to facilitate structured programming). We should now point out that indeed structured programming is easier in some (not all) high-level languages. PL/M for the 8080 is an excellent example, and we devote a brief appendix to a discussion of PL/M and its implementation of structured programming. For the moment, we are assuming that only assembly coding is possible on the system. (The difference in cost between assembler-only and PL/M development systems currently amounts to several thousands of dollars.) The first task in this section, therefore, is to demonstrate precisely why a structured programming control structure is more tricky in assembly language. But then we shall offer a concise procedure for (1) implementing these necessary control structures while, at the same time, (2) avoiding the known pitfalls that await the assembly language programmer.

Any programmer familiar with both a high-level language and an assembly language is well aware of the relative convenience of the former with such expressions as:

```
SUBTRACT DEDUCTIONS FROM GROSSPAY
   GIVING NETPAY    [COBOL]
NETPAY = GROSS - DDCTNS    [FORTRAN]
```

Compare such operations to a similar one implemented in 8080 assembler:

```
CLCNET:                       ; CALCULATE NET PAY
        LDX     H,DDCTNS      ; SET H,L ⟶ AMOUNT OF
                              ; DEDUCTIONS
        LDA     GROSS         ; SET A = GROSS PAY
        SUB     M             ; SUBTRACT DEDUCTIONS
                              ; FROM GROSS AMOUNT
        STA     NETPAY        ; REPLACE NET IN MEMORY
                              ; LOCATION
```

Obviously there is a difference in the degree of convenience between the levels of the languages. But the reader should note carefully that there is absolutely nothing tricky or subtle or counterintuitive about the assembler language implementation; it just takes more instructions by the programmer to accomplish the same thing. By the same token, the longer sequence of instructions in the 8080 code should be as readable as the high-level, single-line instructions. (If the mnemonics for the memory locations have been chosen carefully, as they were in the example, and if the comments are written with readability in mind, then the 8080 sequence should compete favorably in readability.)

But when it comes to program control structures, then it is no longer simply a matter of convenience that the high-level languages are more effective. There is a new element at work that places a special burden on the assembly language programmer. In the case of selection based on test (IF . . . THEN . . . ELSE), coding a block in a structured high-level language is next to trivial:

```
IF SOC.SEC.CUM IS GREATER THAN SOC.SEC.MAX
    MULTIPLY GROSS.PAY BY SOC.SEC.RAT
    GIVING SOC.SEC.DED
ELSE
    MOVE ZEROES TO SOC.SEC.DED.
```

(Theoreticians may argue whether COBOL does indeed implement structured programming properly. It may not in all respects, but it serves well for the examples, at least.) Note that the preceding sequence in COBOL is a realization of the flowchart for selection based on choice (IF . . . THEN . . . ELSE) in Figure 12-1. Observe that there is an almost negligible amount of psychological effort required to recognize the similarity between the flowchart and the high-level language realization of the flowchart. And in addition to actual IF . . . THEN . . . ELSE operators in the language's instruction set, the programmer can enhance readability by uniform indentation of the line. In other words, it is as though the two-dimensional flowchart maintains its two dimensions in the code itself; one almost sees the flowchart reproduced in the code.

Not so in the assembly code version. The implementation of the decision and procedure boxes is left totally up to the programmer. Knowing this, and knowing in particular that the implementation relies upon some critical

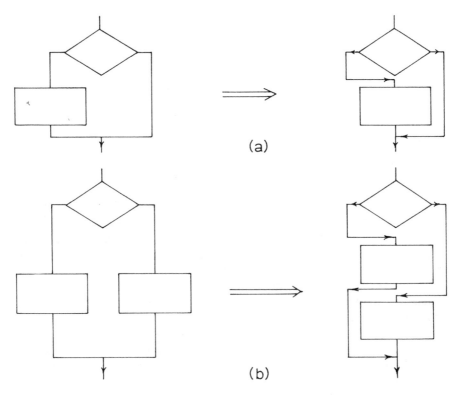

(a)

(b)

Note: The double-lined arrows denote structural transformations.

Figure 12-1. Transformations of IF ... THEN ... (ELSE) Control Blocks

branching in the assembly code, we nudge the flowcharts a little closer to the resulting assembly code by means of the transformation in Figure 12-1. This is more than just an exercise in symbolic manipulation. By placing all of the boxes, both decision and procedure, in vertical alignment, we are forcing the diagram to lose its two-dimensionality and to "look" much like the structure of the assembly code. And the most critical factor for our purposes is the set of paths taken by the single lines. Specifically, a line that proceeds downward and remains on the vertical axis represents simple sequential execution. A line that departs from the vertical axis via a decision box represents a conditional branch. A line that departs from the vertical axis directly represents an unconditional branch. A line (arrowhead) that reconnects with the vertical axis represents a label. Let us now look at some pseudo-code implementations of the preceding flowcharts. Note that this is not high-level code and certainly not the code we would expect to see from a structured programming language.

Structure	High-level p-c	Low-level p-c
IF . . . THEN	If *a* is true,	TEST A
	then do *x*	IF A IS FALSE BRANCH TO ALPHA
		(Block of code for X]
		ALPHA:
		[Block of code for Y]

We should note two characteristics of the preceding implementations. First, the location of branch statements and labels corresponds to the rather formal rules regarding the behavior of the lines and arrowheads of flowcharts, as depicted in Figure 12-1. Second, branching around X occurs in the case of the logical inverse of the condition in the IF statement. We test for true, then branch if false.

The second observation should be transparent to the reader, but this characteristic of testing and branching represents one of the most bothersome features of programming in assembly language. This leads us to the crux of the problem of implementing the IF . . . THEN structure. What begins as an IF . . . THEN in structured programming is normally implemented in assembly code as TEST . . . IF . . . BRANCH (by a structured language compiler), and the condition for branching must be the logical inverse of the condition originally specified in the IF . . . THEN statement.

In the preceding examples we used a general Boolean condition "true" for testing and branching. Let us now focus our attention solely on the first two steps of the implementation: TEST and BRANCH. Bearing in mind that the chief impediment to a smooth transition between the high-level and the low-level implementation of the IF . . . THEN structure is the logical switch between IF TRUE THEN DO X and IF FALSE THEN BRANCH AROUND X, we boldly propose a somewhat radical solution—radical, that is, but nifty, hence to be known hereafter as RAD-NIFTY. This strategy guarantees a virtually effortless translation from (1) English narrative (as in a functional description of a component), to (2) structured pseudo-code, to (3) structured 8080 assembler. Moreover, we claim that the same enhanced readability of the English and pseudo-code will carry over into the 8080 assembler. This may seem too outlandish to be true, and we must hasten to call out the inevitable tradeoffs, even before we sketch out the implementation. These costs may be listed in two parts:

1. A plethora of "bland" labels. In a typical listing, one encounters such colorful statement labels as LOOP, GETNUM, START, and KEEPON, labels that indeed tax the coder's imagination but that nevertheless lend personality to the code itself. In the proposed scheme, we inflict double jeopardy upon code: (a) the labels are artificially contrived in order to denote rigorously the framework of each control block (i.e., each IF . . . THEN . . . ELSE and WHILE . . . DO); (b) the labels are therefore more numerous (and therefore appear to be less necessary) than those in typical assembler code.

2. One "extra" branch instruction per logical test. We mentioned previously that it impedes readability of assembler a great deal for the reader constantly to be forced to shift gears between an IF *a* TRUE . . . (in high-level pseudo-code) to IF *a* FALSE . . . (in low-level pseudo-code) as he or she follows the code. The precise cost of preserving the uninverted truth values of the original IF expressions is 3 (and sometimes 6 or more) bytes of 8080 code per logical test. (We shall see in a moment why this is so.)

By way of brief and immediate rejoinder to each of the preceding objections, we observe first that an increased number of labels results in no visible overhead to the code; that number of labels does not affect the size of the program, nor does it directly affect its speed. As for the second observation, it may very well be that the code for some system is already pushing the limits of the available memory and storage. We know that the limits for microprocessor systems are typically inflexible, inasmuch as the amount of memory is limited to the number of memory chips that will fit into the final package; the cost of the product is also a highly determining factor. If such a limit has been reached for a given system, then 3 (or 6 or more) bytes per logical test is indeed too outrageous a price to pay. However, if memory requirements will allow it, then it would seem to be outrageous (unfortunate, at least) not to invest every prudent effort to enhance and preserve the widest readability and maintainability of the code. Remember those nasty cost curves for hardware versus software and how they get worse every year. Here, then, is the proposed solution for ultimate readability of 8080 assembler.

RAD-NIFTY (Radical-but-Nifty) Coding Conventions

IF . . . THEN *and* IF . . . THEN . . . ELSE

Compare the high-level and the suggested low-level pseudo-code implementation of these structures.

High-level	*RAD-NIFTY*
IF A TRUE	IF010:
THEN	TEST A
DO X	BRANCH TO THN010 IF TRUE
END	BRANCH TO END010 IF FALSE
	THN010:
	CODE FOR X
	END010:

The reader will note immediately the following:

1. The appearance of the control structure is supported by the parallel numbering of the IF*nnn* . . . THN*nnn* . . . END*nnn* set of labels.
2. That same appearance is bolstered by the indentation scheme.
3. Both the IF TRUE branch and the THN*nnn* label (pointing always to the DO IF TRUE code, by our convention) constitute the visible overhead in RAD-NIFTY. The IF*nnn* label is also a convention of RAD-NIFTY that is nonfunctional in the code.
4. The three lines of code addressed by IF*nnn* constitute most (here, all) of the logical testing and branching mechanisms necessary for implementing the control block.
5. To the reader with some ability in assembler coding, the low-level code should resemble assembler very closely. In other words, if RAD-NIFTY appears already to be a readable paraphrase of the high-level statement block, then this is good news for the assembler world.

Let us study a similar comparison for IF . . . THEN . . . ELSE:

High-Level	*RAD-NIFTY*
IF A TRUE	IF020:
THEN	TEST A
DO X	BRANCH TO THN020 IF TRUE
ELSE	BRANCH TO ELS020 IF FALSE
DO Y	THN020:
END	CODE FOR X
	BRANCH TO END020
	ELS020:
	CODE FOR Y
	END020:

As in the case of the preceding IF . . . THEN example, the only "extra" (i.e., purely overhead) code is the IF TRUE line and the THN020 label. And once again the initial IF*nnn* label is added purely for its "framing" effect on the block, unless of course some label at that point might have been necessary to the program anyway.

WHILE . . . DO

Once again, we observe the easy transition from high-level to low-level structured code:

High-Level	*RAD-NIFTY*
WHILE A TRUE	WHL030:
THEN	TEST A
DO X	BRANCH TO THN030 IF TRUE
END	BRANCH TO END030 IF FALSE
	THN030:
	CODE FOR X
	BRANCH TO WHL030
	END030:

The chief difference between this structure and the IF . . . THEN . . . ELSE is that there is a mandatory upward branch at the end of the THEN code of the block. (We assume that something will eventually affect the truth (Boolean) value of *a* in this example, if indeed the programmer ever intended for the iteration eventually to terminate.

Our task for the remainder of this chapter will be to provide the 8080 programmer with the tools necessary to implement the TEST, BRANCH IF TRUE, and BRANCH IF FALSE portions of the control block.

When we "test" some value, we are probably including that value in some sort of logical expression (in the high-level code), which can be categorized according to one of the following:

1. *Equality:* IF A EQUAL B or IF A NOT.EQUAL B. (B in this case may be zero.)
2. *Inequality:* IF A (LESS.THAN / GREATER.THAN / LESS.OR.EQUAL / GREATER.OR.EQUAL) B. (Again, B may be zero.)
3. *Bit settings:* IF MASK (BIT.SET.IN / BIT.CLEAR.IN) A.
4. *Direct interrogation of 8080 flags:* check for any of the following to be high or low: carry, zero, parity, sign.

For the 8080, in particular, the implementation of categories 1 through 3 lies eventually with the carry and zero flags. And we observed at the close of the preceding chapter various permutations of these flags which would indicate these states. The only "trick" now is to determine the precise conditions under which we may rely on the information borne by the carry and zero flags. That is, what instructions must precede our interrogation of these flags? We shall use categories in the preceding list to demonstrate proper sequences of assembler instructions, which include the conditional JUMP instructions of the 8080. And the various examples at the same time will serve as models of RAD-NIFTY, which should be studied in their own right as examples of structured assembler coding.

Test for EQUAL / NOT.EQUAL (Uses zero flag only).

Following DCR **(Decrement) Instruction.** Inasmuch as the DCR in the 8080 assembler is tailor-made for loop control, we shall present here a non-RAD-NIFTY form:

```
          MVI       A,DELAY        ;LOAD ACCUMULATOR WITH
                                   ; DELAY VALUE
LOOP:
          DCR       A              ;DECREMENT THE
                                   ; ACCUMULATOR
          JNZ       LOOP           ;IF ACCUMULATOR STILL NON-
                                   ; ZERO, REPEAT
```

Implementing such a trivial sequence with a full-blown WHILE . . . DO block would be somewhat of an overkill, especially where tight control on timing is necessary. (The formal structured-code version is left as an exercise for the student.) We should caution the reader, however, that not every short sequence of assembler code is logically trivial just because it is short. Wherever readability would be enhanced, we should consider using a structured blocking technique to increase its understandability.

The next example, somewhat less trivial, will demonstrate the readability that results from using a true WHILE . . . DO loop with full-control block structuring. In this example, the task is to increment the first byte of each 5-byte entry in a table consisting of 100 such entries, each 5 bytes wide. Notice especially that although we are incrementing the pointer (by 5) in each iteration, we are decrementing the counter before returning to the top of the WHILE . . . DO loop. This is done in order to query the zero flag which was set or cleared as a result of that decrement. Note also that instruction ORA A (or the accumulator with itself) serves to force the zero flag low (saying, in effect, "the accumulator is not equal to zero").

```
;
; ROUTINE TO INCREMENT FIRST BYTE OF EACH RECORD
;
          MVI D,0            ;SET D,E PAIR FOR DOUBLE-WORD
          MVI E,5            ; INCREMENT VALUE
          MVI A,100          ;INITIALIZE DOWN-COUNTER
          LDX H,TABLE        ;POINT H,L TO 5 X 100 BYTE TABLE
          ORA                ;FORCE ZERO FLAG LOW

WHL040:                      ;WHILE ZERO FLAG IS LOW
          JZ THN040          ; DO THE INCREMENT
          JNZ END040         ; AND EXIT WHEN ZERO FLAG HIGH
```

```
THN040:            ;
  INC M            ;INCREMENT FIRST BYTE OF ENTRY
  ADD L,E          ;ADD FIVE TO LOW BYTE OF POINTER
  ADC H,D          ; AND ADD CARRY TO HIGH BYTE, IF A
                   ; CARRY RESULTED FROM ADD
  DCR A            ;DECREMENT DOWN-COUNTER
  JMP WHL040       ;BACK TO TOP OF LOOP
END040:            ;
```

Note the technique that is necessary to perform a multibyte addition, as we were forced to do when adding 5 to the 2-byte address stored in H,L. The 2-byte 05 is stored in the register pair D,E at the start of the routine.

Once again, with a DCR operation, it may seem that the added baggage of a WHILE . . . DO block is excessive, but note that all the decision-making logic regarding the execution of the loop is forced to the area immediate to the WHL*nnn* label, just where the reader is accustomed to finding it in high-level structured language code.

Following the ORA A Instruction (or the accumulator with itself). This is a means of forcing the zero flag to reveal whether a particular byte is empty or not. The ORA A instruction must in turn be preceded by a MOV, which situates the desired byte into the accumulator, as in the following example:

```
;
; EXECUTIVE ROUTINE TO CALL "SUBR.A" IF THE TICKS
; REMAINING IS GREATER THAN ZERO, CALL "SUBR.B" IF
;     TICKS EQUALS ZERO.
;
; PSEUDO-CODE:
;
;  (1)   IF TKSLFT EQUAL ZERO
;  (2)   THEN
;  (3)      CALL SUBR.A
;  (4)   ELSE
;  (5)      CALL SUBR.B
;  (6)   END
;
          IF050:           ;(1)   (NUMBERS KEYED TO
                                  PSEUDO-CODE)
          LXA TKSLFT       ;      GET TICKS INTO ACCUM.
          ORA A            ;      FORCE  ZERO  FLAG  HI
                                  OR LO
          JZ THN050        ;      ZERO HIGH: ACCUM. = 0
          JNZ ELS050       ;      ZERO LOW: ACCUM. > 0
```

```
THN050:              ;(2)
    CALL SUBR.A      ;(3)
    JMP END050       ;
ELS050:              ;(4)
    CALL SUBR.B      ;(5)
END050:              ;(6)
```

Following CPI (or CMP). In the case of both DCR and ORA above, we were using the zero flag to tell us whether the result was equal to zero or not. With compares we are interested in knowing whether two quantities are equal or not. We found in the last chapter that because of the "hidden" subtraction performed on those two quantities, the zero flag will reveal to a subsequent instruction whether the quantities are equal (zero flag high) or unequal (zero flag low). Consider this example, which tests a memory location (CELL) against a known value (64, decimal) in order to decide which routine (SUBR.A or SUBR.B) to execute:

```
;
; COMPARE MEMORY LOCATION AGAINST A KNOWN QUANTITY
; IN ORDER TO DETERMINE WHICH SUBROUTINE TO CALL
;
; PSEUDO-CODE
; (1)   IF CELL EQUAL 64
; (2)   THEN
; (3)      CALL SUBR.A
; (4)   ELSE
; (5)      CALL SUBR.B
; (6)   END
;
        IF060:           ; (1)
            LDA CELL     ;         GET "CELL" INTO ACCUM.
            CPI 64       ;         DO HIDDEN SUBTRACT
            JZ THN060    ; (1A)    ZERO HIGH: EQUAL
            JNZ ELS060   ; (1B)    ZERO LOW: UNEQUAL
        THN060:          ; (2)
            CALL SUBR.A  ; (3)
            JMP END060   ;
        ELS060:          ; (4)
            CALL SUBR.B  ; (5)
        END060:          ; (6)
```

It should be obvious that if the original pseudo-code statement had been IF ... NOT.EQUAL, then statements 1A and 1B would be reversed in the assembler code.

Test for Inequalities (GREATER.THAN, LESS.THAN, GREATER.OR.EQUAL, LESS.OR.EQUAL)

In order to translate a high-level pseudo-code test phrase containing an inequality into a proper low-level expression, it is necessary to refer to the summary chart of the carry and zero flags. Clearly, the LESS.THAN becomes CARRY.SET and GREATER.OR.EQUAL becomes CARRY.CLEAR. Each of the remaining two inequalities, however, poses an interesting situation from a RAD-NIFTY standpoint.

LESS.OR.EQUAL. The summary chart tells us that this condition is true IF CARRY.SET OR ZERO.SET. The implementation of this expression forces us to introduce an OR label into our RAD-NIFTY repertoire:

```
;
; TEST FOR MEMORY LOCATION TO BE LESS OR EQUAL TO
; KNOWN DECIMAL VALUE
;
; PSEUDO-CODE
;
;(1)    IF CELL LESS.OR.EQUAL 64
;(2)    THEN
;(3)      CALL SUBR.A
;(4)    ELSE
;(5)      CALL SUBR.B
;(6)    END
;
        IF070:              ;(1)
          LDA CELL          ;
          CPI 64            ;
          JC THN070         ;
        OR070:
          JZ THN070         ;
          JNZ ELS070        ;
        THN070:             ;(2)
          CALL SUBR.A       ;(3)
          JMP END070        ;
        ELS070:             ;(4)
          CALL SUBR.B       ;(5)
        END070:             ;(6)
```

Note carefully that the OR*nnn* label in the preceding example is purely for effect. It does not affect branching within the block. It serves only as a visual checkpoint to identify the start of the second half of the logical check.

GREATER.THAN. For this inequality we must implement still another operator, the AND. This is necessary inasmuch as the expression IF . . . GREATER.
THAN must be translated into IF CARRY.CLEAR AND ZERO.CLEAR, according to the inequalities conversion chart. (The reader should convince himself of
this.)

```
;
; ROUTINE TO TEST FOR MEMORY LOCATION TO BE
; GREATER THAN KNOWN DECIMAL VALUE
;
; PSEUDO-CODE
;
;(1)   IF CELL GREATER.THAN 64
;(2)   THEN
;(3)      CALL SUBR.A
;(4)   ELSE
;(5)      CALL SUBR.B
;(6)   END
        IF080:              ;(1)
           LDA CELL         ;
           CPI 64           ;
           JNC AND080       ;
           JC ELS080        ;
        AND080:             ;
           JNZ THN080       ;
           JZ ELS080        ;
        THN080:             ;(2)
           CALL SUBR.A      ;(3)
           JMP END080       ;
        ELS080:             ;(4)
           CALL SUBR.B      ;(5)
        END080:             ;(6)
```

Notice here that the AND label, unlike the OR label in the previous example, is
fully functional, participating in the special branching activity associated with
this particular inequality.

Test for BIT.SET, BIT.CLEAR

The strategy for bit testing in the 8080 is quite straightforward, relying solely
on the ANI instruction to clear unmasked bits and on the zero flag to direct
execution, subsequent to the ANI. Consider an example in which the program

checks the command/status resiger (CSR) of an external device to see whether it is requesting service. Let us assume that CSR bit 4 (where bit 0 is the least significant bit) has been assigned as the "service request" bit.

```
;
; ROUTINE TO POLL DEVICE CSR TO SEE WHETHER
: TO EXECUTE DEVICE SERVICE ROUTINE
:
: PSEUDO-CODE
:
: (1)    IF SERVICE.REQUEST.BIT SET.IN CSR
;(2)    THEN
;(3)        CALL DEVICE SERVICE ROUTINE
;(4)    END
        IF090:                 ;(1)
            IN 1               ;          GET CSR INTO ACCUM.
            ANI SRQMSK         ;          ISOLATE BIT 4
            JNZ THN090         ;          NOT ZERO: BIT IS HIGH
            JZ END090          ;          ZERO: BIT IS LOW
        THN090:                ;(2)
            CALL DEVSRV        ;(3)
        END090:                ;(4)
```

In the preceding example, notice that the immediate data in the ANI instruction is a symbol; it would have previously defined in the program with an EQU or SET directive. Of course, the ANI instruction in the example could also have been written ANI 10000B. However, one very good reason for using symbols instead of absolute values in the code itself is that in case some value needs to be changed, then only the symbol's definition needs to be changed in the source code; symbol definitions will typically be grouped together in a convenient location near the start of the code. In the example, if the absolute binary value had been written in every immediate mode instruction in which it was being used, and if the hardware designers had decided to change the bit assignment in the CSR to bit 7 instead of bit 4, then the programmer would have had to change 10000B to 10000000B in all those instructions. But as a symbol it needs only to be redefined in its EQU statement, and a subsequent reassembly of the code would rectify each of the immediate mode instructions in which the symbol was used.

Use of JMP *and* CALL *Options in the Assembler*

The reason we have gone to such great lengths of elegance in the use of the zero and carry flags in the discussion is that we have been interested not in the flags per se, but in the higher-level semantics of each particular flag. Occasionally, however, the programmer will be very much interested in carry, parity, zero, and sign bits in their own right. In such a situation, the instruction set of the 8080 assembler is rich in its options (JMP, CALL, and RET) which use these flags. The reader should refer to the discussion of the instruction set (which is summarized in Appendix A) and to a programming manual for details. He will find that any JMP, CALL, or RET can be done conditionally, depending on the state of any one of the status flags.

Summary Argument

The reader should be well aware that this chapter constitutes the most controversial portion of the text. We have already listed some possible objections, and there are certainly more. The author's intention has not been simply to inject this piece of originality for its own sake. (Besides, strategies for "hand-assembled" structured code have been published for some years.) The issue here concerns a broader philosophy of programming languages. Any language, whether assembler or high-level, should allow the programmer to devote as much attention as possible to the problem at hand. Conversely, the language should draw as little attention as possible to itself; it should not be "tied" any more than is necessary to the internals of the machine. Although an assembler represents the lowest level in programming languages that can still be called a language, we are arguing that with a handful of conventions even the assembly language programmer can be somewhat liberated to think, design, code, and read source listings in terms of logical control structures and not be totally bound to the level of the processor itself.

A notable breakthrough for microprocessors which addresses itself to all the preceding is the advent of the PL/M programming language for the 8080/8085 family. In the months and years to come, this and other languages will replace assembler as working languages for microprocessor applications. But the pace of that change in the marketplace as a whole will probably be slower than expected, largely because of sheer economics. At the moment of this writing, a development system for PL/M software still costs over $12,000, still out of reach for many users.

RAD-NIFTY is a bargain-basement approach to structured code. It turns the programmer into a compiler (for the control structure blocks). And it is anything but optimized, requiring an extra 3 bytes (at least) for each of the "redundant" jump instructions. But the resulting code is structured, the hardware required is only for the instruction set of the assembler, and the programmer needs only to learn the few "structuring mechanisms" in this chapter in order to conform easily to structured programming standards.

123

Exercises

12-1. Using RAD-NIFTY, convert the pseudo-code in question 11-2 to structured 8080 assembler.

12-2. "Translate" each of these conditional statements to RAD-NIFTY multiline test and execution blocks
   a. IF REG B EQ ACCUM THEN CALL SUBRA ELSE CALL SUBRB
   b. IF REG B NE ACCUM THEN CALL SUBRA ELSE CALL SUBRB
   c. IF REG B GT ACCUM THEN CALL SUBRA ELSE CALL SUBRB
   d. IF REG B LT ACCUM THEN CALL SUBRA ELSE CALL SUBRB
   e. IF REG B LE ACCUM THEN CALL SUBRA ELSE CALL SUBRB
   f. IF REG B GE ACCUM THEN CALL SUBRA ELSE CALL SUBRB

12-3. Now use the same pseudo-code logical operators as in question 12-2 to construct six different WHILE . . . DO blocks, having the following format: WHILE REG B comparison ACCUM CALL SUBRA

13 Some Microprocessor Applications

We have referred occasionally to a design strategy of "top-down implementation." However, we have not really specified what *top* refers to in the real world. In this chapter we shall implement, all the way to the 8080 assembler code level, three microprocessor software components of real products (at least credible products). For each of the components, we shall walk through a miniature design and implementation cycle, in which *top* refers to the initial design requirements or "functional description" of the particular system. The language used at this stage of a product's development is English (or whatever other natural language is used commonly by the customers, marketing people, and designers). As design requirements are brutally and painfully made ever more precise, we see the emergence of *formal specifications*. The medium of expression is still English (or whatever), although the phrasing and vocabulary are "tight" enough now for (1) a designer to use in the implementation of the product and (2) the corporate attorneys to use in possible litigation over patent rights, late delivery schedules, product failure, or whatever other contingency may arise. (Such a prospect should be unlikely, but it emphasizes just how precise specifications must be.)

By the time the designer has formal specifications in hand, a major portion of the design task has been achieved. It is also likely that a large portion of the time alloted for development of the product has elapsed. Project manangers experience their highest blood pressure at this moment, since they observe the anomalous co-occurrence of (1) relaxed smiles on the faces of the software people, and (2) the absence of a single line of computer code. But the designers are smiling because their top-down strategy holds high promise that out of the specifications will "fall" the actual shape of the final computer code; we shall call this as yet nonexecutable shape *pseudo-code*. As a means of catalyzing this fallout, the designer may have drawn a very powerful type of flowchart called a *finite-state diagram*. Naturally, the pseudo-code is structured, so the designer/ programmer has only to translate it into executable computer code, assembler for the 8080 in our case.

We have already hinted that top-down design comprises much more than the consideration of which language or medium is used to convey each step of the process. And we have grossly oversimplified every step. Furthermore, we shall continue to oversimplify as we move through the three design and implementation steps. But oversimplified or not, the general flow from informal product requirements description to executable computer code is a story that

125

should repeat itself for every successful software effort. We leave it to the imagination of the reader to determine where the communications pitfalls are located in this whole process. (The designer who has experienced even a few of these development projects does not need to use his or her imagination, however.) To summarize the cycle for each product, therefore, we shall be watching its development as it is expressed in the language of:

1. Informal requirements definition. What the customer/user expects the system to do, expressed in terms that he and the salespeople can understand, but which may be nonsense (or of little sense) to a pure computer coder.

2. Formal specifications. The language here will still be the native tongue of the user, but he may barely recognize the similarity between this and step 1.

3. Pseudo-code (possibly with finite-state diagrams). The designer/programmer is now moving to the helm. The resulting structured code, although possibly not executable on any known computer, could be easily translated into any high-level structured programming language. (And we know already how a RAD-NIFTY translation works.)

4. Computer code. Only at this "lowest" (a programmer might say "highest") level does the system become bound to a particular computer (unless the language here is portable enough to move from one system to another).

We began this book with the novel statement that the main task is communication, which may have seemed to have little to do with the book's title. But the preceding list bears the heavy implication that the community of people involved in the implementation of a computer-based system must be (collectively) fluent in at least four languages. And where that collective body numbers a single person, as often is the case with low-priority-but-rush projects or in very small companies or departments, then the demands on that person are staggering. Add to these demands the special "language requirements" for real-time systems, in which the programmer must be as conversant as possible in the idiom of hardware design, and we conclude that software designer/coders, especially those involved in real-time systems development, must be renaissance types indeed.

Application A: VMD Mark IV

Functional Description

This will be a voltage monitoring device (VMD). As soon as the input voltage exceeds some predetermined base or threshold voltage for the device being monitored by the VMD, then the computer should set off an audible alarm. That alarm is contained within the external device and can be turned on and off using the same interface circuitry as is used for monitoring the voltage level. Once the alarm is set off, then it should be allowed to continue sounding for a predetermined period of time. After that time has elapsed, then the alarm should be turned off, unless the voltage is still higher than the threshold. If it still exceeds the threshold, then the alarm should continue sounding for that same period of time, after which the voltage will be monitored again, and so on, until the voltage drops below the threshold.

Specifications

1. The microprocessor system shall be so designed that access to and from the control status register shall be through I/O port 1.

2. Excessive voltage (i.e., a voltage level at or above the threshold sensed in the hardware of the external device) shall be flagged by the hardware of the external device to the system as a whole by setting (logical voltage level high) bit 0 of the CSR. When the voltage level is below the established threshold, then bit 0 of the CSR shall be low (= 0).

3. The audible alarm shall be controlled by setting CSR bit 1 to start the alarm and by clearing CSR bit 1 to stop the alarm.

4. The alarm shall begin sounding not more than 1 second past the moment that the external device exceeds the established threshold voltage. That is, no more than 1 second shall elapse between the change in state of CSR bit 0 from low to high and the sounding of the alarm.

5. Once started, the alarm shall continue sounding for 10 seconds (plus or minus 1 second). At the end of that time, the voltage level shall be monitored again (through the CSR) to determine whether or not to clear CSR bit 1 to stop the alarm.

6. The alarm shall remain activated for as long as the input voltage exceeds the threshold (i.e., as long as CSR bit 0 is high).

Finite-State Diagram

As we said earlier, the convention used in writing finite-state diagrams is that each node of the graph represents a state of the system. That state, in turn, may comprise several subtasks to be performed, or it may simply denote a logical transition point in the flow of the total system. Figure 13-1 is a FSD representation of the operation of the VMD. The numbered list describes the activity of each of the correspondingly numbered nodes of the diagram.

Pseudo-Code

Using our own noncomputer mnemonics, we may construct the logic block for the system as follows (using a very high-level pseudo-code):

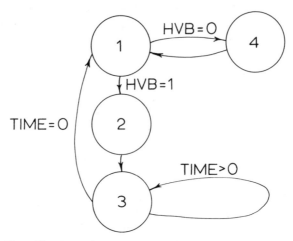

Note: The "states" are described as follows: (1) test for high voltage bit (HVB) set (= 1), (2) start alarm, initialize TIME, (3) decrement TIME, test for TIME = 0, and (4) turn off alarm.

Figure 13-1. Finite-State Diagram (FSD) Representation of Voltage Monitoring Device (VMD)

```
DO FOREVER
   IF HI.VLTG.BIT EQUAL 1
   THEN
      LET ALARM.BIT = 1
      LET TASK.TIMER = ALARM.TIME
      WHILE TASK.TIMER GREATER.THAN 0
         DECREMENT TASK.TIMER
      END
   ELSE
      LET ALARM.BIT = 0
   END
END
```

(The pseudo-code contained as comments in the 8080 assembler listing of this program is written in a somewhat "lower" format than the preceding block.)

8080 Implementation

A full listing of the source code for this routine is shown in Figure 13-2.

```
LOC   OBJ      SEQ    SOURCE STATEMENT

               1    ; TITLE: "VMD": VOLTAGE MONITORING DEVICE
               2    ;
               3    ; AUTHOR: RON TURNER
               4    ; DATE CREATED: 24-FEB-78
               5    ; REVISION INFORMATION:
               6    ;
               7    ;      DATE   REV#    PURPOSE
               8    ;      ----   ----    -------
               9    ;
              10    ;
              11    ; PROGRAM LOGIC (STRUCTURED PSEUDO-CODE)
              12    ;
              13    ;  (1)  WHILE 1 EQUAL 1
              14    ;  (2)    IF HIVLTG EQUAL 1
              15    ;  (3)      LET ALARM = 1
              16    ;  (4)      LET TSKCTR = #TSKTIM
              17    ;  (5)      WHILE TSKCTR GT 0
              18    ;  (6)        DECREMENT TSKCTR
              19    ;  (7)      END
              20    ;  (8)    ELSE
              21    ;  (9)      LET ALARM = 0
              22    ; (10)    END
              23    ; (11)  END
              24    ;
              25    ; NOTES (NUMBERS REFER TO LINES IN PSEUDO-CODE):
              26    ;
              27    ;  (1) A "DO-FOREVER" LOOP
              28    ;  (3) MEANS "SET 'ALARM' BIT IN CSR OF DEVICE.
              29    ;  (4) "TSKCTR" WILL BE THE ACCUMULATOR IN 8080 CODE
              30    ;  (9) WITH 'ALARM' BIT IN CSR ALREADY CLEARED IN (2) BY "ANI" INSTRUCTION,
              31    ;      WE MERELY WRITE THE CSR BACK TO ITSELF.
              32    ;
              33    ;
              34    ;
00FF          35    TSKTIM  EQU   0FFH
0001          36    HIVMSK  EQU   01H         ;BIT 0 OF CSR (HIGH VOLTAGE BIT)
0002          37    ALRMSK  EQU   02H         ;BIT 1 OF CSR (ALARM BIT)
              38    ;
0004          39            ORG   04
              40
              41    VMD:
              42    IFU10:                     ;(1)
0004 D801     43            IN 1               ;(2)
0006 E601     44            ANI HIVMSK         ;    ISOLATE BIT ZERO IN ACCUMULATOR
0008 C20E00   45            JNZ THN010
000B CA1800   46            JZ ELS010
              47    THN010:
000E F602     48            ORI ALRMSK         ;(3)  SET BIT 1 IN CSR
0010 D301     49            OUT 1              ;(4)
0012 3EFF     50            MVI A,TSKTIM       ;(5)
              51
              52    LOF010:
```

Figure 13-2. Code for VMD.

```
LOC  OBJ      SEQ         SOURCE STATEMENT

0014 3D        53         DCR  A              ; (6)
0015 C21400    54         JNZ LOPO10          ; (7)
               55
0018 D301      56  ELSO10:                    ; (8)
               57         OUT 1               ; (9)
001A C30400    58  ENDO10:                    ; (10)
               59         JMP VMD             ; (11)
               60
               61  END

PUBLIC SYMBOLS

EXTERNAL SYMBOLS

USER SYMBOLS
ELSO10 A 0018    ENDO10 A 001A   HIVMSK A 0001   IF010 A 0004   LOPO10 A 0014   THNO10 A 000E
ALRMSK A 0002
TSKTIM A 00FF    VMD  A 0004

ASSEMBLY COMPLETE, NO ERRORS
```

Figure 13–2. *Continued*

Application B: SEKUR-T (Device for Building Security)

Functional Description

After opening the outside door, the user (in this case, the person using his or her key to enter the building) has a given number of seconds to reach the keyboard entry station. The number of seconds is predetermined, and the location of the station is to be known only by privileged occupants of the building. Upon reaching the station, the person must press the proper key on a 10-digit keyboard. If the correct digit is entered, then nothing happens. If the wrong digit is entered, then there is a lapse of time (also predetermined) before the alarm is activated. Only a single digit may be entered, and that digit must be entered correctly the first time. If the person does not even reach the keyboard entry station within the originally alotted time, then the alarm is automatically activated. (Later versions of the product will offer some obvious features of flexibility—a sequence of keys may be specified, instead of a single one; a setable number of retries; etc.

Specifications

1. The system interface shall be through the CSR accessed through I/O port 1.
2. Within the system CSR, bit 0 is the status of the outside door lock (1 = locked, 0 = unlocked).
3. CSR bit 15 controls the alarm (1 = activate alarm, 0 = deactivate alarm).
4. One additional register, known as BUTTON REGISTER, shall be accessed through I/O port 2. The 10 low-order bits in that register correspond to the 10 keys on the keypad. This register can be both read and written to by the microprocessor (write capability necessary in order to clear the register).
5. The microprocessor system shall be driven by a 2-microsecond clock.
6. The maximum time between bit 0 of the system CSR going from high to low and the setting of a single bit in BUTTON REGISTER (equals BTN.REG in the pseudo-code below) shall be 7 seconds.
7. The time interval between entering the wrong digit and the activation of the alarm (false assurance interval) shall be 3 seconds.

The reason for the slow system clock in the specifications is to make possible as lengthy a wait as is possible, using only a single-byte down-counter. The implementation of a double-byte counter, and therefore a longer wait, is more complicated and will not be treated here. (The problem is that the zero flag is not affected in a DCX instruction, as it is in a DCR.)

Pseudo-Code

```
DO FOREVER
   WHILE DOOR.LOCKED.BIT SET.IN CSR
   END
   LET TIMER = SLOW.TIME
   WHILE TIMER GREATER.THAN 0 AND BTN.REG EQUAL 0
      DECREMENT TIMER
   END
   IF TIMER GREATER.THAN 0 AND GOOD.BTN SET IN BTN.REG
   THEN
      WHILE DOOR.LOCKED.BIT CLEAR.IN CSR
      END
      LET BTN.REG = 0
   ELSE
      LET TIMER = FAST.TIME
      WHILE TIMER GREATER.THAN 0
         DECREMENT TIMER
      END
      LET CSR = CSR SET.BY ALARM.MASK
   END
END
```

Note that the two WHILE loops, which contain no code, are really "wait" loops, waiting in this case for the condition tested in the WHILE expression to change. This change will occur externally. The WHILE's that contain a DECREMENT are "delay" loops, in which the condition being tested by the WHILE will be modified within the loop itself.

8080 Assembler Implementation

Figure 13-3 is the listing for this program. Again, note the pseudo-code at the head of the comments, together with the "notes" that refer both to the pseudo-code and to the actual assembler code.

Application C: The TRAU-MATIC Mark IV

We must begin this application—which represents a pedagogical grand finale of sorts—by disclaiming the reality of the product we are about to build. It is not that the 8080 is incapable of serving as the microprocessor base of the system, nor that the reader is by now incapable of developing the software for such a

```
LOC OBJ   SEQ   SOURCE STATEMENT

           1  ;  TITLE: SECURE (SECURITY/ALARM DEVICE)
           2  ;
           3  ;
           4  ;  AUTHOR: RON TURNER
           5  ;  DATE CREATED: 24-FEB-78
           6  ;  REVISION INFORMATION:
           7  ;      DATE    REV#      PURPOSE
           8  ;      ----    ----      -------
           9  ;
          10  ;
          11  ;  PROGRAM LOGIC (STRUCTURED PSEUDO-CODE)
          12  ;
          13  ;  (1)  SECURE:
          14  ;  (2)      WHILE 1 EQUAL 1
          15  ;  (3)          WHILE DORLKD EQUAL 1
          16  ;               END
          17  ;  (5)          INITIALIZE WLKTIM = SLOTIM
          18  ;  (6)          WHILE WLKTIM GREATER 0 AND BUTTON REGISTER CLEAR
          19  ;  (7)              DECREMENT WLKTIM
          20  ;  (8)              CHECK BUTTON REGISTER
          21  ;  (9)          END
          22  ; (10)          IF WLKTIM GREATER 0 AND "GOOD BUTTON BIT" SET IN BUTTON REGISTER
          23  ; (11)              WHILE DORLKD EQUAL 0
          24  ; (12)              END
          25  ; (13)          ELSE
          26  ; (14)              DELAY FASTIM
          27  ; (15)              SOUND ALARM
          28  ; (16)          END
          29  ; (17)      END
          30  ; (18)  END
          31  ;
          32  ;  NOTES (NUMBERS REFER TO PARENTHISIZED NUMBERS IN PSEUDO- AND 8080 CODE):
          33  ; (2,17)  A "DO-FOREVER" LOOP
          34  ; (3)     THE DOOR KEY ACTUALLY SETS AND CLEARS A BIT IN THE CSR (WHICH IS
          35  ;         ACCESSED TEROUGH I/O PORT 1 IN THE HARDWARE
          36  ;         THIS LOOP IS EXECUTED FOR AS LONG AS THE DOOR REMAINS LOCKED.
          37  ; (3,4)   "BUTTON REGISTER" IS AN EIGHT-BIT BIT MAP, ONE BIT FOR EACH OF THE
          38  ;         BUTTONS SCATTERED THROUGHOUT THE ENTRY AREA. ONLY ONE BUTTON IS
          39  ; (6)     DESIGNATED AS "GOOD". THE BUTTON REGISTER IS ACCESSED THROUGH
          40  ;         I/O PORT 2.
          41  ; (10)    "GOOD BUTTON" IS DEFINED AS A MASK WITH A SINGLE BIT SET
          42  ; (11,12) LOOP EXECUTED AS LONG AS DOOR IS UNLOCKED (LAWFULLY!)
          43  ; (14)    A THREE-SECOND INTERVAL WILL ELAPSE BETWEEN PUSHING THE WRONG
          44  ;         BUTTON AND THE SOUNDING OF THE ALARM.
          45  ; (15)    SOUNDING ALARM PERFORMED BY SETTING BIT 15 IN CSR
          46  ;
          47  ;
          48  ;
          49     SECOND EQU 36     ;NUMBER OF ITERATIONS THROUGH NOP LOOP TO
          50                       ;ACHIEVE 1 SECOND DELAY, USING 2-MICROSEC CLOCK:
          51                       ;  LOOP:
0024      52                       ;      NOP
```

Figure 13-3. Code for Security System

```
LOC    OBJ       SEQ   SOURCE STATEMENT            COMMENT

00FC             53    SLOTIM EQU 7 * SECOND       ; JMP LOOP
006C             54    FASTIM EQU 3 * SECOND       ;7 SECONDS' "SLOW TIME" FOR GETTING TO BUTTON
                 55                                ;3 SECONDS BEFORE ALARM SOUNDS ON ILLEGAL CONDITION
                 56
0080             57    ALARM  EQU 10000000B        ;BIT 15 HIGH IN CSR ACTIVATES ALARM
0001             58    DORLKD EQU 00000001B        ;BIT ZERO IN CSR INDICATES STATE OF LOCK
0010             59    GUDBTN EQU 00010000B        ;BIT FOUR IN BUTTON REGISTER IS ONLY VALID ONE
                 60
0000             61    ORG 0                       ;O.K. TO START IN LOW READ-WRITE MEMORY
                 62                                 ;(NO INTERRUPT VECTORS HERE)
                 63    SECURE:
                 64    LOP010:                      ;(1)
                 65                                 ;(2)
                 66
0000 DB01        67    LOP020:
0002 E601        68            IN 1
0004 C2000U      69            ANI DORLKD
                 70            JNZ LOP020            ;(3)
                 71
0007 06FC        72    MVI B,SLOTIM                 ;(4)
                 73
0009 05          74    LOP030:
000A CA1300      75            DCR B
000D DB02        76            JZ END030            ;(6)
000F B7          77            IN 2                 ;(7)
0010 CA0900      78            ORA A
                 79            JZ LOP030
                 80    END030:                      ;(9)
                 81
0013 78          82    IF010:
0014 B7          83            MOV A,B
0015 CA2C00      84            ORA A
0018 DB02        85            JZ ELS010
001A E610        86            IN 2
001C C22200      87            ANI GUDBTN
001F CA2C00      88            JNZ THN010
                 89            JZ ELS010
                 90    THN010:
                 91
0022 DB01        92    LOP040:
0024 E601        93            IN 1
0026 CA2200      94            ANI DORLKD
                 95            JZ LOP040            ;(12)
                 96
0029 C33600      97            JMP END010           ;(13)
002C 3E6C        98    ELS010:                      ;(14)
                 99            MVI A,FASTIM
                 100
002E 3D          101   LOP050:
002F C22E00      102           DCR A
                 103           JNZ LOP050
                 104
0032 3E80        105           MVI A,ALARM          ;(15)
0034 D301        106           OUT 1                ;(16)
                 107   END010:
```

; (5)
; (8) GET BUTTON REGISTER INTO ACCUMULATOR
;   SET OR CLEAR Z FLAG TO CHECK FOR EMPTY
; (10) START OF COMPOUND "IF" STATEMENT
;   SET OR CLEAR Z FLAG TO CHECK FOR ZERO TIME
;   CHECK FOR VALID BUTTON
; (11)

Figure 13-3. *Continued*

```
LOC  OBJ        SEQ         SOURCE STATEMENT

0036 C30000     108    JMP LOPO10           ;(17)
                109    END                  ;(18)

PUBLIC SYMBOLS

EXTERNAL SYMBOLS

USER SYMBOLS
ALARM  A 0080    DORLKD A 0001    ELSO10 A 002C    END010 A 0036    END030 A 0013    FASTIM A 006C    GUDBTN A 0010
IFU10  A 0013    LOPO10 A 0000    LOPO20 A 0000    LOPO30 A 0009    LOPO40 A 0022    LOPO50 A 002E    SECOND A 0024
SECURE A 0000    SLOTIM A 00FC    THNO10 A 0022

ASSEMBLY COMPLETE, NO ERRORS

ISIS-II ASSEMBLER SYMBOL CROSS REFERENCE, V2.0

ALARM    57#   105
DORLKD   58#    69    94
ELSO10   65     69    98#
END010   97    107#
END030   76     80#
FASTIM   55#    99
GUDBTN   59#    87
IFU10    82#
LOPO10   65#   108
LOPO20   67#    70
LOPO30   74#    79
LOPO40   92#    95
LOPO50  101#   103
SECOND   49#    54    55
SECURE   64#
SLOTIM   54#    72
THNO10   88     90#

CROSS REFERENCE COMPLETE

Ready
```

Figure 13-3. *Continued*

system, it is rather because of some simple economic tradeoff considerations that the TRAU-MATIC Mark IV will probably never be seen in the marketplace. Just why we are about to present a rather ample design and coding walkthrough of such a system will be discussed shortly.

Briefly, the TRAU-MATIC Mark IV is to be newest entry in the line of products known as "intelligent" computer terminals. Although intelligence in a computer is difficult to describe and measure in a positive manner, we can easily cite the most widely known type of nonintelligent terminal: the teletype. This bottom-of-the-line computer terminal is able to accept and decode characters as they are entered by the user, to transmit those characters to the computer, to receive characters back from the computer, and to present those characters to the user in a medium that he or she can understand. Typically, the characters are entered by physical depression of typewriter-like keys, and the received characters (both those echoed from the keyboard and those received from the computer) are written onto paper by impact from a printing hammer or character cylinder. But the (one-time) use of paper is certainly not the speediest nor the most cost-effective means of writing character data. Instead of paper, a terminal could just as well echo and print characters on a CRT screen. A terminal which is functionally as simple as a teletype but which utilizes a CRT instead of paper (known generically as a "glass teletype") is another example of a nonintelligent computer terminal.

But the moment that the medium changes to something as transient (and therefore as speedy) as the phosphor-coated screen of the CRT, some design enhancements immediately suggest themselves. The *rate* of printing out characters is no longer bound by the limitation of the speed of the firing hammer of the teletype; whole lines of text, even a whole page (screen's worth) of text can be printed out in seconds or a fraction of a second. The *order* of printing characters is now free from the strict left-to-right sequence of the teletype; any character may be printed anywhere on the screen regardless of the location of the previous character. And when paper and ink are no longer the media, then characters can be erased, or whole lines can be erased, or the entire remainder of a page can be erased, beginning from a given location on the page, or the whole page can be erased. There is one serious drawback to the glass teletype which in turn suggests even a further enhancement to the total system: when the screen becomes filled with text, then whatever was on the screen will have been scrolled out of view. (With paper hard copy, the user merely has to reach for the "scrolled-out" segment and it will be found, perhaps several yards distant from the teletype and amidst a pile of paper rubble, but it will be found.) A feature of the intelligent terminal could be to allow the user to view whole pages selectively, scrolling the text forward or backward, without the computer's having to retransmit each page to be viewed. Finally, and perhaps most dramatic of all, the limitation to English alphanumeric characters is no limitation at all in an intelligent CRT terminal. There could be several options of languages, even those requiring exotic font styles. But there is nothing sacred about letters and numbers; the screen can easily depict geometric shapes, graphs, and even different colors.

All the features we have just described exist in currently marketed intelligent computer terminals. These features place certain demands on the system, as evidenced by their various prices. Graphics and color capability certainly require more sophisticated hardware, in addition to the sizable effort in software. But for any degree of added intelligence (beyond that required for the teletype), we can expect a need for a larger keyboard, added data storage capacity within the terminal itself, and a microprocessor that executes some carefully designed software (which in turn demands its own storage).

Overview of Software Requirements

The president of FAH-ROUT Systems, Inc., Mr. Nixon Wyres, is no dummy. He has personally witnessed the rise and demise of over a dozen computer systems companies in the past 10 years. He was, in fact, dismissed from his previous job, in which he designed a disk interface which for each unit required seven printed circuit boards and 515 IC chips. (At that time he felt strongly that microprocessors were only a passing fad, that all software people were strange, and that the world could be made safe for democracy using only AND and NOR gates.) When his disk interface proved impossible to troubleshoot and service, even in the development laboratory, he was fired. But a beneficent neighbor lady handed him a paid tuition scholarship to a microprogramming course in Vunnysale, California. There he learned that anything that hardware can do, software can do better and maybe cheaper, since after all, writing instructions costs nothing, while making circuit boards costs a pretty penny.

Consequently, when Mr. Wyres formed his own company, he resolved that the only IC chips he would allow in his products would be those whose functions could absolutely not be accomplished by the microprocessor.

All the preceding background material is necessary to explain the software requirements of the TRAU-MATIC Mark IV.

A fledgling company, FAH-ROUT was certainly in no position to afford separate personnel for marketing, product management, requirements definition, plus all the necessary engineering and fabrication positions. It should therefore be no surprise to the reader that Mr. Wyres himself was responsible for formalizing the requirements of the product, all the way down to the level of identifying the major tasks of the software to run the system. (Fortunately, he did not attempt to develop the software personally; he ran a full-page ad in *Computerworld* to find the best software engineer that money could buy.) And Wyre's memos were always to be understood as the final word, no matter how absurd his design suggestions seemed to his software engineer.

His memo of software task distribution for the **TRAU-MATIC** Mark IV specified the following.

Null Task. Whenever the microprocessor is not busy doing something else, then it should show that it is alive and well by turning the cursor on the screen off and on at a rate to be determined by the software engineer. Mr. Wyres, who at the ripe age of 26 can recall the days when computers always created some visible commotion when they were running, disliked the notion of a tiny, low-heat-producing, hidden IC chip doing its thing without at least flashing a light somewhere. (During his infamous tenure with the disk interface project, he dedicated an entire printed circuit board's worth of hardware logic to an animated LED display on a front panel of the disk unit which spelled out HEY! I'M ALIVE! and then gave Greenwich Mean Time, local temperature, and relative humidity.)

Background Tasks. These tasks are the real meat of the product. The features to be included are:
   1. Cursor addressing and control. Not only can the cursor be moved by the operator, but under program control as well, the cursor can be moved right, left, up, down, to the start of the next line, or to the home (upper left corner) from any position on the screen. The cursor is totally addressable; therefore the cursor can be moved immediately to any coordinate on the screen. All this makes true graphics possible on the terminal.
   2. Erase capability. Options here include: (a) erase the remainder of a line, beginning at the location of the cursor; (b) erase the remainder of the screen, beginning at the cursor; (c) erase the entire screen, no matter where the cursor is located, and move the cursor to the home position.
   3. Scrolling capability. At any time the operator can "bring back" a previous page (screen's worth) of text, or "bring up" successive pages, a whole screen's worth at a time.
   4. Local editing capability. Without assistance from the host computer, the operator will be able to add, change, or delete characters in any line of text. When a page has been altered to the operator's satisfaction, then the whole page can be sent off to the host computer to be substituted.

Foreground Tasks. Whatever else this terminal may be able to do—and the Mark V, Mark VI, etc. will be able to do more—it must always be a terminal that is able to "talk" to a host computer. The two primary functions of the system therefore are:

1.   To transmit characters to the host computer. Since the TRAU-MATIC will always "know" when it has characters to send, when it is sending those characters, and when it has finished sending those characters, this portion

of the foreground logic will not be interrupt-driven. (We shall expand on this in some detail during the design discussion.)

2.   To receive characters from the host computer. Unlike the procedures for transmitting characters, the terminal does not "know" precisely when a character is to be received. The receiving logic will therefore be written in an interrupt-driven mode; the terminal's microprocessor system will be interrupted and "told" when a character is being transmitted from the host computer. The terminal's own logic therefore does not have to be constantly checking (= polling) to see whether a character is on the way.

Communications: The Major Problems

The area of computer communications represents an entire field of study in electrical engineering and computer science and is the focus of intense activity at the present time, thanks to the upsurge of decentralized processing. No longer are computer designers (as a whole) striving to build bigger and mightier *mainframes* (stand-alone computer systems), but the trend now is to build sophisticated *networks,* in which computing power is distributed more evenly between a host computer and satellite computers or between several host computers and their satellites. And even an example as hypothetical as the intelligent terminal which we are about to explore brings us very abruptly to two of the fundamental issues of computer communications: (1) serialization and deserialization of data, and (2) communications protocol. These issues have a direct bearing on the portion of the TRAU-MATIC we are to design, so we must understand clearly the problems involved and the types of design decisions necessary.

Serialization and Deserialization of Data. Let us assume the fundamental unit of data to be the *character.* And to simplify matters, let us adopt the standard of the ASCII character set, in which all alphanumeric and even some purely functional and nonprintable characters are represented by an octal number within the range 0 to 177. In selecting this standard, we are agreeing to a character set each of whose members can be uniquely represented by 7 bits: 0 (octal) = 0 000 000 (binary); 177 (octal) = 1 111 111 (binary). The problem of how to transmit data can now be stated with greater precision: how do we send characters over a line, 7 bits at a time? We know that in the computation process, we need think only of characters when we consider the smallest unit of a message (assuming that the word length of the computer is at least 7 bits). We read in characters, compare characters, concatenate characters, and write characters back out to memory, all without being conscious of individual bits within the characters. This is made possible because of the internal architecture of the computer, which performs its moves and logical functions in a parallel fashion. In a move, for example, it is as though each bit of the source register or memory location were physically tied (connected) to the corresponding bit of the destination register or memory location. In the 8080 instruction

    MVI   A,101Q   ;MOVE "A" TO THE ACCUMULATOR

the octal code for A (= 101) is moved into the accumulator. The architecture of the 8080 is such that the 8 bits specified in the data position of the command (1 000 001 (binary)) are moved in parallel fashion into the accumulator. Bit 0 of the data byte is moved into bit 0 of the accumulator, bit 1 of the data is moved into bit 1 of the accumulator, and so on.

It would be simple from a design standpoint if actual data transmission outside the computer could also be accomplished in a parallel (bit-for-bit) fashion. But the requirements for such a mode of transmission are obvious and absurd, at least where real, physical lines are concerned. Whenever data needed to be sent between computers, it would require (at least) seven separate lines; this would either rule out the use of voice-grade telephone lines for data communication or would require seizing at least seven separate lines, all going between the same two points, whenever an ASCII message was to be sent. The most readily available alternative is for the data to be sent bit-by-bit instead of bit-for-bit. That is, the 7-bit parallel ASCII character is serialized into a sequence of successive bits, and these bits are transmitted, one after the other, over the data transmission line. At the receiving end, the other computer accumulates the bits as they arrive and converts the bit stream back into a parallel ASCII character which can then be processed internally. This parallel-to-serial-to-parallel process is fundamental to any communications system which relies on single lines (or other bit-at-a-time communications channels) for data transmission.

Communications Protocol. We have already pointed out the importance of protocol in any system that incorporates separate subsystems, each with its own internal timing mechanisms. And the protocol required for data communication is perhaps the most elegant to be found anywhere. Fortunately, since by its very nature this area demands cooperation and standardization, there are now some widely accepted schemes, one of which we shall follow in the design.

It is conceptually easy for us to picture the character A coming over a data line. But the picture becomes somewhat blurred when we realize that the A will actually be the sequence of data bits 1-0-0-0-0-0-1. And if the letters ABC were to be sent to us back-to-back the bit stream would be 1-0-0-0-0-0-1-0-1-0-0-0-0-1-1-0-0-0-0-1. Add to this confusion the reality of occasional noise on the line (bits indiscriminately set high) and we suddenly find ourselves in dire need of something more than bit-by-bit transmission of characters. If we were receiving the characters "by hand" (assuming we could receive the bits fast enough), we would need some assurance that the first "high" bit of a bit stream was really part of a character and not just some line noise. Then we would like to know that when we think that a character's transmission is complete, it really is complete. Finally, it would be best to have some means of verifying that the 7 bits of data we received were in fact the same 7 bits sent by the transmitting computer. Solutions to these (and other) problems comprise the topic of *communications protocol.* Let us examine one particular strategy that accomplishes all the wishes just expressed.

The strategy we are about to present is used in most systems in which the transmission rate is relatively slow, as is the case in most communication between terminals and their host computers. The strategy is called *asynchronous,* and since the basic design is best explained by the actual layout of the bit stream, we shall refer to its implementation as the *asynchronous format.* We shall look first at a timing diagram (or waveform) and then point out some aspects of the asynchronous scheme that constitute intelligent "assumptions" on the part of both receiver and transmitter (study Figure 13-4).

Assumptions.

1. Before transmission, the line will always be left in the 1 position. This may actually be implemented by the line voltage's being positive as opposed to negative, or by the current's being on as opposed to off.

2. The rate of transmission and, therefore, the individual bit and character times will be known by both processors in advance.

3. Each bit will require its full "bit time" (minus the time needed for transition from and to the surrounding bits).

Protocol.

1. The line goes low, indicating a possible START bit. The receiving processor samples the line to be certain that it stays low, signifying that this is indeed a valid bit and not a burst of line noise.

2. The first character bit is sent and received during the bit-time DB0. The remaining 6 character bits occur during their respective bit times.

Figure 13-4. Wave Form for Asynchronous Data Transmission

3. If the system is set to do parity checking, then the bit-time DB7 is used for the parity bit. Depending on the convention accepted, bit 8 will be high or low if the sum of bits 1 through 7 is even; this is called *odd* or *even* parity, respectively.

4. A full bit time's worth of 1 must be received to signify "end of character" (STOP) as the end of the current character's bit stream.

The software development task in the TRAU-MATIC will be to design and code the portion of the foreground task that is to transmit and receive data. These functions are precisely the functions performed by the class of logic components known generically as the UART (for Universal Asynchronous Receiver/Transmitter). (If the reader has not guessed the origin of the product's name, he or she should by all means do so at once.) As a matter of engineering fact, it is not likely that the ordinary designer (without the eccentricities of Nixon Wyres) would opt for a software implementation of a UART. It is simply too inexpensive not to incorporate as a separate chip, and the chip is available from several manufacturers. But the author should at least justify why he chose to subject the reader to this somewhat hypothetical application.

1. As mentioned before, the original cost per chip is not the whole story in the fabrication process; since placing chips on a circuit board also accounts for real costs. Although saving chip costs in an intelligent terminal would be somewhat of a savings overkill, it should never be dismissed without at least some serious consideration. (The exercise could certainly be called "serious consideration.")

2. A microprocessor (and a very powerful one at that) is already being used in the system, and very little of its time will be used for executing the background (feature) tasks of the system. Operators are human, and humans type and read slowly. Since the microprocessor is there anyway and is idle most of the time, why not put it to work on other necessary tasks?

3. A microprocessor is totally programmable (no news to any software person). This means that in revisions of the product, the UART functions can be modified as easily as other portions of the software.

4. This project is a fair illustration of the notion of virtually concurrent foreground/background/null activity within a single processor.

5. Both hardware and software types can gain some mutual appreciation. Programmers can learn something of the hardware involved in a typical UART, and the hardware types can see how their shift registers and delays, for example, are "emulated" in software. (We are not attempting to do a gate-by-gate emulation of the hardware, however.)

Functional Description (Receive Task Only)

The receive portion of the TRAU-MATIC will be interrupt-driven, meaning that it will begin execution only when the first bit of a serialized bit stream reaches the device. It will assume data to be in an asynchronous format, meaning that each bit time is assumed to be of uniform duration. After the first bit has been verified by the receive task to be a legitimate data bit and not just a "spike" of line noise, the remaining data bits are deposited, in order, in a named memory location. A flag is checked at this time to be sure that the previously received byte has been read by the other portion of the program; if it has not, then an OVERRUN ERROR is flagged. Also at this time, the receiver task sets a flag to notify the rest of the system that a new byte has been deserialized and is in the named memory location waiting to be read. Other error conditions are FRAMING (the absence of a STOP bit following the eighth data bit, and PARITY (an unmatched PARITY bit, as calculated by the receiver and compared to the parity bit that was received from the sender).

Specifications

1. The transmission format shall be asynchronous, with single start and stop bits, and a parity bit for odd parity check.

2. The processor clock shall generate a clock cycle every 480 nanoseconds.

3. The transmission rate shall be set initially at 1200 baud (bits per second).

4. The input data line shall be connected directly to bit 0 of the input data register.

5. The entire receive task shall be interrupt-driven, the interrupt to be generated by the input data line's transition from low to high logic level.

6. To verify that the interrupting bit is valid, a check for "high" on the data line shall be performed one-half a bit time following the interrupt.

7. With interrupts still disabled, the 7 data bits and the parity bit shall be received and deposited into a predetermined memory location.

8. Odd parity shall be assumed; that is, a high parity bit specifies that an odd number of ones were sent in this transmission. If the parity bit does not match the parity check as made by the receive task, then a PARITY ERROR shall be flagged in the CSR (bit 0).

9. In the event that a proper STOP bit is not received following the 7 data bits and the parity bit, then a FRAMING ERROR shall be flagged in the CSR (bit 1).

10. If the receive task determines (by finding the RECEIVER EMPTY bit of the CSR (bit 2) to be low) that the previous data word was not processed by the system, then the receive task shall flag an OVERRUN ERROR in the CSR (bit 4).

11. When the receive task has finished deserializing the data byte, it shall set the DATA ALL READ bit in the CSR (bit 3).

12. Interrupts to the system shall be re-enabled only after the entire task has been completed or until the receive task determines that the initial incoming bit was simply line noise and not real data.

For the pseudo-code and 8080 assembler implementation, see the listing in Figure 13-5.

Compared to the receive task, which must be interrupt-driven, the design and implementation of the transmit portion is simple, largely because it can be coded as a polling operation.

```
LOC   OBJ      SEQ       SOURCE STATEMENT

                1    ; TITLE: "RCVISR": RECEIVE INTERRUPT SERVICE ROUTINE
                2    ;                  (COMPONENT OF "SOFTWARE UART" FOR 8080)
                3    ;
                4    ;
                5    ; AUTHOR: RON TURNER
                6    ; DATE CREATED: 20-JAN-78
                7    ; REVISION INFORMATION:
                8    ;       DATE     REV#     PURPOSE
                9    ;       ----     ----     -------
               10    ;       21-APR   RT1      INITIALIZE CSR
               11    ;
               12    ;
               13    ; PROGRAM LOGIC (STRUCTURED PSEUDO-CODE)
               14    ;
               15    ;   (1)    DELAY .5 BIT-TIME (LOP010)
               16    ;
               17    ;   (2)    IF INCOMING BIT STILL LOW (IF NOT JUST NOISE)
               18    ;   (2.5)    INITIALIZE CSR (CLEAR ERROR BITS, READY FLAG)     ;RT1
               19    ;   (3)      INITIALIZE BIT COUNTER
               20    ;   (4)      INITIALIZE PARITY ACCUMULATOR
               21    ;
               22    ;   (5)      WHILE BIT.COUNT GT 0 (LOP020)
               23    ;   (6)        DELAY BIT-TIME (LOP030)
               24    ;   (7)        ADD INCOMING BIT TO PARITY ACCUMULATOR ("PARSUM")
               25    ;   (8)        MOVE BIT INTO PARALLEL BYTE ("RCVBYT")
               26    ;   (9)        DECREMENT BIT.COUNT
               27    ;  (10)      END
               28    ;
               29    ;  (11)      IF INCOMING BIT (PARITY) DOES NOT MATCH "PARSUM"
               30    ;  (12)        SET PARITY ERROR BIT IN CSR
               31    ;  (13)      END
               32    ;
               33    ;  (14)      DELAY BIT-TIME (LOP040)
               34    ;
               35    ;  (15)      IF INCOMING BIT NE STOP (1)
               36    ;  (16)        SET FRAMING ERROR BIT IN CSR
               37    ;  (17)      END
               38    ;
               39    ;  (18)      IF "RECEIVER EMPTY" BIT NOT HIGH IN CSR
               40    ;  (19)        SET OVERRUN ERROR BIT IN CSR
               41    ;  (20)      END
               42    ;
               43    ;  (21)      SET "RECEIVER READY" BIT HIGH IN CSR
               44    ;  (22)    END
               45    ;
               46    ;
               47    ; NOTES:
               48    ;
               49    ;   (2):  THE TYPICAL CSR FUNCTIONS ARE PERFORMED IN THE MEMORY LOCATION
               50    ;         "CSR" AND NOT THROUGH AN I/O PORT.
               51    ;   (1),(6),(14): EACH DELAY ASSURES THAT SAMPLING OF THE DATA LINE WILL OCCUR
               52    ;         NEAR THE MIDDLE OF THE DATA BIT'S STEADY STATE
```

Figure 13-5. Code for Software UART.

```
LOC   OBJ      SEQ      SOURCE STATEMENT

               53   ;
               54   ; (2),(7),(15); INCOMING BIT IS TIED TO BIT 0 OF THE INPUT PORT. THE BIT IS
               55   ;      ISOLATED BY "ANI" IN THE ACCUMULATOR
               56   ;
               57   ; (7):  THE EXCLUSIVE-OR INTO "PARSUM" PERFORMS SINGLE-BIT-WIDTH ADDITION OF
               58   ;       DATA BIT INTO LEAST SIGNIFICANT BIT
               59   ;
               60   ; (8):  THE SERIAL-TO-PARALLEL CONVERSION UTILIZES THE CARRY FLAG AS A TEMPORARY
               61   ;       STORAGE LOCATION FOR THE INCOMING DATA BIT
               62   ;
               63   ; (11): THE CHECK FOR PARITY ERROR MOVES THE LAST BIT RECEIVED (PARITY BIT) TO THE
               64   ;       LEAST SIGNIFICANT POSITION OF THE ACCUMULATOR, ISOLATES THAT BIT, THEN COM-
               65   ;       PARES WITH THE LSB OF "PARSUM". ON ERROR, "CSR" HAS ITS PARITY ERROR BIT
               66   ;       SET. THE CHECK HERE ASSUMES CHECK FOR ODD PARITY.
               67   ;
               68   ; (16): THE OVERRUN CHECK VERIFIES THAT THE PREVIOUS PARALLEL CHARACTER HAS
               69   ;       BEEN READ OUT OF THE "RCVBFR" LOCATION BY THE PROCESSOR. THE STATUS OF
               70   ;       "RCVBFR" IS FLAGGED IN THE "RECEIVE BUFFER EMPTY" FLAG OF THE CSR.
               71   ;       THE "BACKGROUND" PROGRAM SETS THE BIT HIGH WHEN IT HAS MOVED A CHARACTER
               72   ;       FROM THE BUFFER, AND THE INTERRUPT SERVICE ROUTINE DROPS THE BIT TO 0
               73   ;       WHEN IT DEPOSITS A CHARACTER INTO THE BUFFER. THIS DOUBLE-BUFFERING
               74   ;       SCHEME PERMITS THE PREVIOUS CHARACTER TO REMAIN INTACT, EVEN IF A BAD
               75   ;       TRANSMISSION ALLOWS A BAD CHARACTER INTO "RCVBYT".
               76   ;
               77   ; (21): THE EXIT ROUTINE SETS APPROPRIATE FLAGS IN THE CSR, THEN RETURNS EXECUTION
               78   ;       TO THE CODE IN LOW MEMORY.
               79   ;
               80   ; SYMBOL DEFINITIONS
               81   ; BITS IN CSR:
0001           82   PARMSK   EQU   00000001B      ;BIT 0:  PARITY ERROR
0002           83   FRMMSK   EQU   00000010B      ;BIT 1:  FRAMING ERROR
0004           84   RMTMSK   EQU   00000100B      ;BIT 2:  RECEIVER EMPTY   (WRITTEN BY MAIN PROGRAM)
0008           85   RCVRDY   EQU   00001000B      ;BIT 3:  RECEIVER READY   (SET BY THIS ROUTINE)
0010           86   OVRMSK   EQU   00010000B      ;BIT 4:  OVERRUN ERROR
               87   ;
               88   ; OTHER SYMBOLS:
0008           89   BITCTR   EQU   08             ;BIT COUNTER FOR LOOP
               90   ;
               91   ; CALCULATED VALUE FOR DELAY LOOP COUNTER (TO ASSURE PROPER WAIT FOR BIT-TIME
               92   ; TO ELAPSE BETWEEN SAMPLINGS)
               93   ;
01E0           94   CYCTIM   EQU   480                  ;# NANOSECONDS PER CYCLE TIME
0007           95   ITRTIM   EQU   (15 * CYCTIM) / 1000 ;# MICROSECONDS PER ITERATION OF LOOP
               96   ;                                   ;LOOP IS OF THE FORM:
               96   ;                                   ;LABEL:
               97   ;                                   ;           DCR   REG    (5  MICROSECONDS)
               98   ;                                   ;           JNZ   LABEL  (10 MICROSECONDS)
               99   ;
000C          100   BAUDRT   EQU   12                   ;BAUD RATE DIV. BY 100
2710          101   SECOND   EQU   10000                ;# MICROSECONDS (/100) IN 1 SECOND
0341          102   BITTIM   EQU   SECOND / BAUDRT      ;# MICROSECONDS IN 1 BIT-TIME
0077          103   FULDLY   EQU   BITTIM // ITRTIM     ;# ITERATIONS OF LOOP FOR 1 BIT-TIME
003B          104   HLFDLY   EQU   FULDLY / 2           ;"  "  "  "  .5  "
              105   ;
              106   ; A "RST 0" INSTRUCTION, ISSUED BY PERIPHERAL DEVICE, WILL TRANSFER EXECUTION
              107   ;
```

Figure 13-5. Continued

```
LOC   OBJ          SEQ   SOURCE STATEMENT

                   108   ; TO LOCATION 08H IN LOW MEMORY. THE CODE LOCATED HERE WILL:
                   109   ;    (1) CALL THE INTERRUPT SERVICE ROUTINE
                   110   ;    (2) RE-ENABLE INTERRUPTS AFTER THE ROUTINE IS COMPLETED
                   111   ;    (3) RETURN EXECUTION TO THE SEQUENTIAL CODE THAT WAS INTERRUPTED
                   112   ;        BY THE EXTERNAL DEVICE.
                   113   ;
0008               114         ORG   08H               ;THIS LOCATES THE FOLLOWING CODE IN LOW MEMORY
0008  CD4000       115         CALL  RCVISR            ; (1)
000B  FB           116         EI                      ; (2)
000C  C9           117         RET                     ; (3)
                   118   ;
                   119   ; THE INTERRUPT SERVICE ROUTINE IS CALLED IN ORDER TO RECEIVE A SINGLE CHAR-
                   120   ; ACTER, BIT-BY-BIT, AND THEN TO PLACE THAT CHARACTER INTO AN EIGHT-BIT
                   121   ; MEMORY LOCATION ("RCVBYT") IN PARALLEL FORM.
                   122   ;
                   123   ;
                   124   ; AFTER CHECKING INITIALLY FOR LINE NOISE, ADDTIONAL ERROR CHECKING IS PER-
                   125   ; FORMED FOR PARITY AND FRAMING ERRORS AND FOR A DATA OVERRUN CONDITION.
                   126   ;
                   127   ; THE INTERRUPT IS GENERATED BY A TRANSITION OF THE DATA LINE FROM 1 TO 0.
                   128   ;
                   129
0040               130         ORG   40H
                   131   RCVISR:
0040  213B00       132         LXI   H,HLFDLY          ; (1)
0043  4E           133         MOV   C,M
                   134
                   135   LOP010:
0044  0D           136         DCR   C
0045  C24400       137         JNZ   LOP010
                   138
                   139   IF010:
0048  3A0008       140         IN    1                 ; (2)
004A  E604         141         ANI   01H
004C  CA5200       142         JZ    THN010
004F  C2C600       143         JNZ   END010
                   144   THN010:
0052  3A0008       145         LDA   CSR               ; (2.5)
0055  E604         146         ANI   RMTMSK            ;CLEAR ALL BUT "RECEIVER EMPTY"
0057  320008       147         STA   CSR               ; (3)
005A  0608         148         MVI   B,BITCTR          ; (4)
005C  210208       149         LXI   H,PARSUM
005F  3600         150         MVI   M,0
                   151
                   152   LOP020:
0061  217700       153         LXI   H,FULDLY          ; (5)
0064  4E           154         MOV   C,M
                   155
                   156   LOP030:
0065  0D           157         DCR   C                 ; (6)
0066  C26500       158         JNZ   LOP030
                   159
0069  DB01         160         IN    1                 ; (7)
006B  E601         161         ANI   01H
006D  210208       162         LXI   H,PARSUM
```

Figure 13-5. *Continued*

```
LOC   OBJ      SEQ  SOURCE STATEMENT

0070  AE       163          XRA   M              ; (8)
0071  320208   164          STA   PARSUM
0074  DB01     165          IN    1
0076  1F       166          RAR
0077  210108   167          LXI   H,RCVBYT
007A  7E       168          MOV   A,M
007B  1F       169          RAR
007C  77       170          MOV   M,A            ; (9)
007D  05       171          DCR   B              ; (10)
007E  C26100   172          JNZ   LOP020
               173
               174  IF020:                       ; (11)
0081  17        175          RAL
0082  17        176          RAL
0083  E601      177          ANI   01H
0085  210208    178          LXI   H,PARSUM
0088  AE        179          XRA   M
0089  C28F00    180          JNZ   THN020
008C  CA9700    181          JZ    END020
               182
008F  3A0008   183  THN020:  LDA   CSR            ; (12)
0092  F601     184          ORI   PARMSK
0094  320008   185          STA   CSR
               186
0097  217700   187  END020:  LXI   H,FULDLY       ; (13)
009A  4E       188          MOV   C,M             ; (14)
               189
               190  LOP040:
009B  0D       191          DCR   C
009C  C29B00   192          JNZ   LOP040
               193
               194  IF030:                        ; (15)
009F  DB01     195          IN    1
00A1  E601     196          ANI   01H
00A3  C2A900   197          JNZ   THN030
00A6  CAB100   198          JZ    END030
               199
00A9  3A0008   200  THN030:  LDA   CSR            ; (16)
00AC  F602     201          ORI   FRMMSK
00AE  320008   202          STA   CSR
               203
               204  END030:                       ; (17)
               205  IF040:
00B1  3A0008   206          LDA   CSR             ; (18)
00B4  E604     207          ANI   RMTMSK
00B6  CABC00   208          JZ    THN040
00B9  C2C100   209          JNZ   END040
               210
00BC  3A0008   211  THN040:  LDA   CSR            ; (19)
00BF  F610     212          ORI   OVRMSK
               213
00C1  F60B     214  END040:  ORI   RCVRDY         ; (20)
00C3  320008   215          STA   CSR             ; (21)
               216
00C6  C9       217  END010:  RET                  ; (22)
```

Figure 13-5. *Continued*

```
LOC   OBJ         SEQ           SOURCE STATEMENT

                  218  ;
                  219  ; READ/WRITE DATA DEFINITIONS
0800              220         ORG     800H        ;START OF 3RD K OF MEMORY
0800 00           221  CSR:    DB      00H         ;THE MEMORY STORAGE LOCATION OF THE CSR
0801 00           222  RCVBYT: DB      00H         ;RECEIVE DATA BUFFER
0802 00           223  FARSUM: DB      00H         ;PARITY SUM ACCUMULATOR
                  224         END
```

PUBLIC SYMBOLS

EXTERNAL SYMBOLS

USER SYMBOLS
```
BAUDRT A 000C   BITCTR A 0008   BITTIM A 0341   CSR    A 0800   CYCTIM A 01E0   END010 A 00C6   END020 A 0097
END030 A 00B1   END040 A 00C1   FRMMSK A 0002   FULDLY A 0077   HLFDLY A 003B   IF010  A 0048   IF020  A 0081
IF030  A 009F   IF040  A 00B1   ITRTIM A 00B1   LOP010 A 0044   LOP020 A 0061   LOP030 A 0065   LOP040 A 009B
OVRMSK A 0010   PARMSK A 0001   PARSUM A 0802   RCVBYT A 0801   RCVISR A 0040   RCVRDY A 0008   RMTMSK A 0004
SECONL A 2710   THN010 A 0052   THN020 A 008F   THN030 A 00A9   THN040 A 00BC
```

ASSEMBLY COMPLETE, NO ERRORS

Figure 13-5. *Continued*

14 Integration and Testing

Throughout this book we have pointed out the various distinguishing characteristics of real-time design and programming. But there is nothing in the world of software to compare with the moment of the "marriage" between some piece of real-time software and the device it is to control. This high degree of uniqueness probably accounts for the inability of the average data processing person to fit well into real-time activity.

But first a scenario. Six months of intense design activity have elapsed, during which both software and hardware people have communicated with marketing people and with each other. Ideally, everyone concerned has generated document after revised document (each one dated and properly entered into the project file). However, because this project was declared by management to be "practically trivial" and utilizing off-the-shelf software and hardware "with just a few modifications here and there," the project received neither sufficient priority nor sufficient budget and manpower to enable appropriate design meeting and review session time. Many corners were cut, since, after all, this project had to be sandwiched in among other more pressing priorities. The mode of intergroup communication was mainly that of (literally) cornering someone in the hallway on his way to coffee, and most of the major design and redesign decisions continued unwritten, undocumented, undated, and unfiled. But the software people and the hardware people did their work in spite of it all, and each of them finished his work ahead of the scheduled delivery time. "It is ready to ship, then?" asked the worried project coordinator one afternoon, just five working days before the scheduled shipping date. "Just about," responded the optimistic designers in cheerful unison. "We only have to hook it all up in the lab."

None of the personnel in this organization seems to be aware of a pernicious disease that lurks among nearly all technical and professional personnel. The author chooses to call it the law of interdisciplinary mutual admiration (IMA). The organizations afflicted with the syndrome rarely recognize it as a problem or hazard because it poses as a benign attribute rather than the terminal malignancy it really is. In plain English, IMA syndrome describes the state of mind and heart of a person in one discipline (software engineering, for example) who assumes that people with comparable rank and experience in another discipline (electronic systems, for example) really know what they are doing. This is probably akin to the generous practice of assuming innocence until proven guilty. In very practical terms, the novice software engineer (who, naturally, is

151

aware of his own deficiencies) assumes that the hardware device dreamed up and built by the hardware designer will operate as the designer said it would, since, after all, hardware is hardware and "those guys know what they're doing." (If the logic of this sentence eludes the reader, he should ignore it; the same sequence is played out in real life, whether logical or not.) However, the hardware designer knows that software makes it possible to take "words" (in the English sense) and transform them so gracefully and effortlessly into real, executable logic, since that is his job. And since the software engineer said that his program would drive the device in such-and-such a manner ("He *did* say that, didn't he . . . or was it the other way around?"), then certainly the program will work. And anyway, if it doesn't work, the software engineer can recode it fast to get it working. "Those software people can really do magic with code, mostly because it's so easy to create programs out of thin air."

Act two of the scenario opens in the laboratory where integration is about to take place. Three of the five days scheduled for integration and testing have been consumed by endless searches for proper circuit boards (and then for properly functioning circuit boards), power supplies, extension cords, cables, plugs, and getting the software physically moved into position (read-only memory chips, disks, or tapes). Then, with the company president overseeing this jubilant ceremony of inauguration, someone pushes the START button and nothing happens. The president remembers an important phone call he must make, and leaves after 10 minutes; "Hang in there, fellas!" he encourages them.

Soon everyone concerned and knowledgeable about the newborn system has surrounded it with microprocessor analyzers, logic analyzers, probes, oscilloscopes, voltmeters, and whatever else the lab has available. At 10:34 P.M. someone is heard to exclaim, "But I thought *you* would clear that bit before I sent you another word." To which another responds, "No, no, no! You told me you would send the byte first and then *you* would clear the bit, remember?" "Yeah, but that was before we changed our minds. Remember just before we went home early for New Year's and I told you . . . ?" And on and on it goes. And that accounts for integration bug number 1. Before the system is finally shipped, the bedraggled group will have plowed through 28 such known bugs before the president decrees to "button it up" just to avoid a lawsuit for late delivery. And before six calendar months have elapsed, three design engineers will have spent 24 man-months (including overtime) plus much airfare dealing with problems with the product in the field.

The preceding melodrama will appear entertaining only to students who have never suffered through the ordeal of making a totally new hardware/software package work. As the practice of software engineering for real-time systems begins to mature, the phase known as *system integration* begins also to develop first some guidelines that ultimately will mature into a subdiscipline in its own right. In this brief chapter, we shall simply list a few such guidelines and then present a model for system integration which may in turn stimulate thinking about even more efficient models.

Following are a few words meant to minimize the inevitable bloodshed that will occur during real-time system integration:

1. At all costs, maintain a sense of humor. If someone on the integration team has lost his sense of humor, send him home to bed. (He probably will have been working 47 hours nonstop.) If he cannot be sent home, then import a comedian to offset the nastiness. There is probably no effort within the engineering department that demands such delicate interpersonal relationships. Everyone must learn to accept blame, ridicule, and accusations, false and true, and yet to respond with a gracious, humble smile.

2. Everyone must drop all defensiveness. The integration phase is no time for a headstrong virtuoso to prove himself right, if there is the slightest possibility, no matter how hypothetical, that he may have made an error or a mistaken assumption. The simple economics of the integration process dictates that the number of man-hours is multiplied by the number of people involved. So no one should impede the progress of the whole group unnecessarily.

3. Do everything possible to ensure that the bugs which surface at this time are "integration bugs" and not trivial "intraroutine" logic bugs. With a carefully designed, modular software system, it should be possible for the programmer to enter the integration phase with internal logic fully checked out. Again, it is outrageous to hold up the entire team while some programmer seizes the entire testing facility to debug some ASCII-to-decimal conversion routine, something that could have been done strictly on his own time in a stand-alone mode.

4. Assume from the outset that the designers in the "other" group (hardware, if you are in software) will make the same number of unfounded and undocumented assumptions and design decisions that you will make over the development of the product. In other words, recognize and counteract the IMA syndrome from the outset. The project coordinator should *demand* that any considerations that could possibly affect system integration progress be deliberated on and properly documented.

5. Allow a disinterested outsider to play "devil's advocate" with the new system in the design requirements phase. In real-time systems, this means asking as many naive and probing questions as possible: What happens to all those decision tables when the power goes down? What if the user does not type the key he is supposed to type? What if a telephone repairman mistakenly cuts the communication line between the host and satellite processor for a brief interval? These are all very real situations that will ultimately be tested during the integration and testing phase; they are conditions that should be deliberately designed for from the outset.

6. Schedule a ridiculous amount of time for integration and testing. Integration bugs typically require an order of magnitude more time to rectify than intramodule logic bugs. It is not unreasonable for a single moderately difficult bug to require most of a man-month to remove from a system at this stage.

Anyone who has experienced system integration could add many more suggestions to this list. But let us turn now to a suggested model for a system integration project. Specifically, this is a proposed strategy for allocating personnel and extracting bugs from a system in a relatively orderly manner. The order of events in the outline below describes identifiable subtasks in a looping algorithm. The letter at the right of each subtask line identifies the people involved: (1) G: entire design group; (2) S: subgroup (software group only, or possibly just two out of the whole integration effort, for example); (3) L: Lone Ranger (one qualifies to be a Lone Ranger by having been the primary or secondary designer of a component that has been positively identified as the source of a bug).

A. Debugging
    1. Isolation of offending routine(s)   S
    2. Isolation of exact erroneous logic, code,
       structures   L
B. Recoding
    1. Informal (oral) description of solution   G
    2. Formal writing of code   L
    3. Minidesign review of written code   G
    4. Editing, recompilation, physical transfer
       of revised software and listing(s)   S
C. Testing
    1. Primary testing over area(s) formerly
       deficient, as per A   S
    2. Comprehensive testing of all known
       features of the software system   S
D. Go to A

The intent of the strategy we propose in the preceding model is to prevent wasted activity either by attempting to deluge the integration activity with too many bodies or by abandoning a single designer/programmer, no matter how knowledgeable, to a bug hunt into any and all areas of the system.

In summary, the integration phase of real-time systems must assume from the outset that neither hardware nor software will be functional at first. Second, it must expect to discover that even when the two components are functioning there will be further "integration bugs" that are generated purely because of interface phenomena. We should inject every design feature possible into the system such that possible hardware-software interface problems may be diagnosed and resolved as easily as possible. And finally, the allocation of personnel during the integration phase must be "fine tuned" such that the proper people, and only the necessary people, are dedicated to the project at each step.

Appendix A
Instruction Set for 8080A
Assembler

Summary of Processor Instructions

Mnemonic	Description	Mnemonic	Description
Move, Load, and Store		SPHL	H & L to stack pointer
MOV*r1, r2*	Move register to register	LXI SP	Load immediate stack
MOV M,*r*	Move register to memory		pointer
MOV *r*,M	Move memory to register	INX SP	Increment stack pointer
MVI*r*	Move immediate register	DCX SP	Decrement stack pointer
MVI M	Move immediate memory		
LXI B	Load immediate register	**Jump**	
	Pair B & C	JMP	Jump unconditional
LXI D	Load immediate register	JC	Jump on carry
	Pair D & E	JNC	Jump on no carry
LXI H	Load immediate register	JZ	Jump on zero
	Pair H & L	JNZ	Jump on no zero
STAX B	Store A indirect	JP	Jump on positive
STAX D	Store A indirect	JM	Jump on minus
LDAX B	Load A indirect	JPE	Jump on parity even
LDAX D	Load A indirect	JPO	Jump on parity odd
STA	Store A direct	PCHL	H & L to program
LDA	Load A direct		counter
SHLD	Store H & L direct		
LHLD	Load H & L direct	**Call**	
XCHG	Exchange D & E, H & L	CALL	Call unconditional
	Registers	CC	Call on carry
		CNC	Call on no carry
Stack Ops		CZ	Call on zero
PUSH B	Push register Pair B & C	CNZ	Call on no zero
	on stack	CP	Call on positive
PUSH D	Push register Pair D &	CM	Call on minus
	E on stack	CPE	Call on parity even
PUSH H	Push register Pair H &	CPO	Call on parity odd
	L on stack		
PUSH PSW	Push A and Flags on	**Return**	
	stack	RET	Return
POP B	Pop register Pair B &	RC	Return on carry
	C off stack	RNC	Return on no carry
POP D	Pop register Pair D &	RZ	Return on zero
	E off stack	RNZ	Return on no zero
POP H	Pop register Pair H &	RP	Return on positive
	L off stack	RM	Return on minus
POP PSW	Pop A and Flags off	RPE	Return on parity even
	stack	RPO	Return on parity odd
XTHL	Exchange top of stack,		
	H & L		

155

Mnemonic	Description	Mnemonic	Description
Restart		SBI	Subtract immediate from
RST	Restart		A with borrow
Increment and Decrement		**Logical**	
INR *r*	Increment register	ANA *r*	And register with A
DCR *r*	Decrement register	XRA *r*	Exclusive Or register
INR M	Increment memory		with A
DCR M	Decrement memory	ORA *r*	Or register with A
INX B	Increment B & C	CMP *r*	Compare register with A
	registers	ANA M	And memory with A
INX D	Increment D & E	XRA M	Exclusive Or memory
	registers		with A
INX H	Increment H & L	ORA M	Or memory with A
	registers	CMP M	Compare memory with A
DCX B	Decrement B & C	ANI	And immediate with A
DCX D	Decrement D & E	XRI	Exclusive OR immediate
DCX H	Decrement H & L		with A
		ORI	Or immediate with A
Add		CPI	Compare immediate
ADD *r*	Add register to A		with A
ADC *r*	Add register to A with		
	carry	**Rotate**	
ADD M	Add memory to A	RLC	Rotate A left
ADC M	Add memory to A with	RRC	Rotate A right
	carry	RAL	Rotate A left through
ADI	Add immediate to A		carry
ACI	Add immediate to A	RAR	Rotate A right through
	with carry		carry
DAD B	Add B & C to H & L		
DAD D	Add D & E to H & L	**Specials**	
DAD H	Add H & L to H & L	CMA	Complement A
DAD SP	Add stack pointer to	STC	Set carry
	H & L	CMC	Complement carry
		DAA	Decimal adjust A
Subtract			
SUB *r*	Subtract register from	**Input/Output**	
	A	IN	Input
SBB *r*	Subtract register from	OUT	Output
	A with borrow		
SUB M	Subtract memory from A	**Control**	
SBB M	Subtract memory from A	EI	Enable Interrupts
	with borrow	DI	Disable Interrupt
SUI	Subtract immediate from	NOP	No-operation
	A	HLT	Halt

Note: the 8080 assembler mnemonics are copyrighted by the Intel Corporation and are used here and throughout the text by permission of Intel.

Table B-1
Hexadecimal-Decimal Conversion Table

	0	1	2	3	4	5	6	7	8	9	A	B	C	D	E	F
000	0000	0001	0002	0003	0004	0005	0006	0007	0008	0009	0010	0011	0012	0013	0014	0015
010	0016	0017	0018	0019	0020	0021	0022	0023	0024	0025	0026	0027	0028	0029	0030	0031
020	0032	0033	0034	0035	0036	0037	0038	0039	0040	0041	0042	0043	0044	0045	0046	0047
030	0048	0049	0050	0051	0052	0053	0054	0055	0056	0057	0058	0059	0060	0061	0062	0063
040	0064	0065	0066	0067	0068	0069	0070	0071	0072	0073	0074	0075	0076	0077	0078	0079
050	0080	0081	0082	0083	0084	0085	0086	0087	0088	0089	0090	0091	0092	0093	0094	0095
060	0096	0097	0098	0099	0100	0101	0102	0103	0104	0105	0106	0107	0108	0109	0110	0111
070	0112	0113	0114	0115	0116	0117	0118	0119	0120	0121	0122	0123	0124	0125	0126	0127
080	0128	0129	0130	0131	0132	0133	0134	0135	0136	0137	0138	0139	0140	0141	0142	0143
090	0144	0145	0146	0147	0148	0149	0150	0151	0152	0153	0154	0155	0156	0157	0158	0159
0A0	0160	0161	0162	0163	0164	0165	0166	0167	0168	0169	0170	0171	0172	0173	0174	0175
0B0	0176	0177	0178	0179	0180	0181	0182	0183	0184	0185	0186	0187	0188	0189	0190	0191
0C0	0192	0193	0194	0195	0196	0197	0198	0199	0200	0201	0202	0203	0204	0205	0206	0207
0D0	0208	0209	0210	0211	0212	0213	0214	0215	0216	0217	0218	0219	0220	0221	0222	0223
0E0	0224	0225	0226	0227	0228	0229	0230	0231	0232	0233	0234	0235	0236	0237	0238	0239
0F0	0240	0241	0242	0243	0244	0245	0246	0247	0248	0249	0250	0251	0252	0253	0254	0255

Appendix C
PL/M Code for Software UART Routine

```
PL/M-80 COMPILER    RECEIVE INTERRUPT SERVICE ROUTINE
ISIS-II PL/M-80 V3.0 COMPILATION OF MODULE RCVISR
OBJECT MODULE PLACED IN :F1:RCVISR.OBJ
COMPILER INVOKED BY:  PLM80 :F1:RCVISR.PLM DEBUG DATE(24-APR-78)
                $TITLE ('RECEIVE INTERRUPT SERVICE ROUTINE')
                $XREF
    1           RCVISR:
                DO;

                /***** I/O DEFINITIONS AND MASKS *****/

    2     1     DECLARE PORT1 LITERALLY              '08H';
    3     1     DECLARE HLFDLY LITERALLY             '57';
    4     1     DECLARE FULDLY LITERALLY             '114';
    5     1     DECLARE CSRVAL LITERALLY             '800H';
    6     1     DECLARE OVRMSK LITERALLY             '08H';
    7     1     DECLARE PARMSK LITERALLY             '00H';
    8     1     DECLARE FRMMSK LITERALLY             '01H';
    9     1     DECLARE RMTMSK LITERALLY             '02H';
   10     1     DECLARE RCVRDY LITERALLY             '04H';
   11     1     DECLARE BIT$CNTR LITERALLY           '08H';
   12     1     DECLARE PARITY$BIT LITERALLY         '80H';
   13     1     DECLARE NEW$BIT LITERALLY            '80H';

   14     1     DECLARE PARSUM BYTE;
   15     1     DECLARE RCV$BYTE BYTE;
   16     1     DECLARE CSR BYTE;

                /* SOFTWARE VARIABLES */

   17     1     DECLARE A BYTE;
   18     1     DECLARE B BYTE;

                $EJECT
   19     1     DO WHILE 1;                          /* CONTINUE FOREVER */

   20     2       DO A = 0 TO HLFDLY-1;              /* HALF DELAY LOOP */
   21     3       END;                               /* END OF HALF DELAY */

   22     2       IF (1 AND INPUT(PORT1)) <> 0 THEN DO; /* IF NO NOISE ON LINE */
                                                      /* PERFORM THE UART FUNCTION */

   24     3         PARSUM = 0;                      /* RESET PARITY */
   25     3         RCV$BYTE = 0;                    /* CLEAR BYTE HOLD AREA */
   26     3         CSR = ((CSR AND RMTMSK) OR CSRVAL); /* INITIALIZE */

   27     3         DO A = 0 TO BIT$CNTR-1;          /* GET 8 BITS OF DATA */

   28     4           DO B = 0 TO FULDLY-1;          /* DO A FULL DELAY LOOP */
   29     5           END;                           /* END OF FULL DELAY LOOP */

   30     4           PARSUM = ((INPUT(PORT1)AND 1) XOR PARSUM);
                                                     /* SET IN PARITY BIT */
   31     4           RCV$BYTE = (ROR(INPUT(PORT1),1) AND NEW$BIT) OR (ROR(RCV$BYTE,1));
                                                     /* SET IN NEW BIT IN HOLD BYTE */
   32     4         END;                             /* END OF GETTING 8 BITS */

   33     3         IF ((INPUT(PORT1) AND 1) XOR (ROL(PARSUM,1))) <> 0
                      THEN CSR = CSR OR PARMSK;      /* SET PARITY ERROR IF NECESSARY */

   35     3         DO A = 0 TO FULDLY-1;            /* DO A FULL DELAY LOOP */
   36     4         END;                             /* END OF FULL DELAY LOOP */

   37     3         IF (INPUT(PORT1) AND 1) <> 0
                      THEN CSR = CSR OR FRMMSK;      /* CHECK STOP BIT AND IF IN ERROR */
                                                     /* SET FRAMING ERROR */

   39     3         IF (CSR AND RMTMSK) = 0
                      THEN CSR = CSR OR OVRMSK;      /* IF RECEIVER EMPTY SET OVERRUN FLG */

   41     3         CSR = CSR OR RCVRDY;             /* SET RECEIVER READY BIT */

   42     3       END;                               /* END OF NO NOISE   */
   43     2     END;                                 /* END OF DO WHILE */
   44     1     END RCVISR;                          /* END OF SOFTWARE MODULE */
```

Note: PL/M is the property of the Intel Corporation, and this example code is included here by permission of Intel.

159

PL/M-80 COMPILER   RECEIVE INTERRUPT SERVICE ROUTINE
CROSS-REFERENCE LISTING

DEFN	ADDR	SIZE	NAME, ATTRIBUTES, AND REFERENCES
17	0003H	1	A BYTE
			20 27 35
18	0004H	1	B BYTE
			28
11			BITCNTR LITERALLY
			27
16	0002H	1	CSR BYTE
			26 34 38 39 40 41
5			CSRVAL LITERALLY
			26
8			FRMMSK LITERALLY
			38
4			FULDLY LITERALLY
			28 35
3			HLFDLY LITERALLY
			20
			INPUT BUILTIN
			22 30 31 33 37
	0000H		MEMORY BYTE ARRAY(0)
13			NEWBIT LITERALLY
			31
8			OVRMSK LITERALLY
			40
12			PARITYBIT LITERALLY
7			PARMSK LITERALLY
			34
14	0000H	1	PARSUM BYTE
			24 30 33
2			PORT1 LITERALLY
			22 30 31 33 37
15	0001H	1	RCVBYTE BYTE
			25 31
1	0000H	210	RCVISR PROCEDURE STACK=0002H
10			RCVRDY LITERALLY
			41
9			RMTMSK LITERALLY
			26 39
			ROL BUILTIN
			33
			ROR BUILTIN
			31

MODULE INFORMATION:
    CODE AREA SIZE   = 00DCH   220D
    VARIABLE AREA SIZE = 0005H   5D
    MAXIMUM STACK SIZE = 0002H   2D
    70 LINES READ
    0 PROGRAM ERROR(S)
END OF PL/M-80 COMPILATION

Answers to Selected Exercises

Chapter 3

3-2.   Designate a "summary error" bit which, then set, signals only that some specific error bit is set elsewhere in the CSR.

Chapter 4

4-1.   (b) 0FEH, 254; (d) 0A3H, 163
4-2.   (b) 131, 83H; (d) 199, 0C7H
4-3.   (b) 10100101, 0A5H; 10100111, 0A7H; (d) 10101001, 0A9H; 10101000, 0A8H
4-4.   (b) 00001010, 0AH; 00011010, 1AH

Chapter 6

6-2.   (a) MASK0   EQU   00000001B   ;BIT 0
             MASK1   EQU   00000010B   ;BIT 1
             MASK2   EQU   00000100B   ;BIT 2
6-4.   ITERAT EQU TOTDLY/LOPTIM
6-5.   DEVTBL: DS   4 * 5   ;DEFINES SPACE ONLY
6-6.   TABLE 2:   DB   0,0,0,0   ;INITIALIZES ALL BYTES
                  DB   0,0,0,0   ; TO ZERO
                  DB   0,0,0,0
                  DB   0,0,0,0
                  DB   0,0,0,0

Chapter 7

7-2.   LHLD   DATSAV   ;SET H,L ⟶ "DATSAV"
       MVI   M,0FH   ;HEXADECIMAL
       MVI   M,15   ;DECIMAL
       MVI   M,17Q   ;OCTAL

Chapter 8

8-2.   (b)   IN   1   ;INPUT CSR

161

```
                        ANI        10000000B        ;ISOLATE BIT 7
                        CNZ        FLGERR           ;IF NOT ZERO, CALL ERROF
                                                    ; ROUTINE
          (d)           IN         1                ;INPUT CSR
                        ORI        00000001B        ;SET ALARM BIT IN CSR
                        OUT        1                ;OUTPUT UPDATED CSR
8-3.      (b)           STA        WHOZIT           ;STORE ACCUM
                                                    ; (CONTAINING
                                                    ; PLAYER NO.)
                        CALL       VERNUM           ;VERIFY THIS
                                                    ; NUMBER AS
                                                    ; BEING PART OF
                                                    ; ROSTER
                        IN         1                ;INPUT CSR
                        JNC        NMBROK           ;CARRY CLEAR =
                                                    ; "THAT PLAYER
                                                    ; WAS O.K."
                        ORI        10000000B        ;SET BIT 7
                        JMP        OUTCSR           ;
          NMBROK:
                        ANI        011111111B       ;CLEAR BIT 7
                                                    ; (OTHER BITS
                                                    ; UNAFFECTED)
          OUTCSR:
                        OUT        1                ;OUTPUT CSR
```

Chapter 9

```
9-1.   (a)   MVI        A,15         ;LET ACCUM = 15
             ADI        14           ;ADD 14 TO ACCUM
             STA        SUM          ;STORE ACCUM IN MEMORY
       (b)   MVI        A,15         ;LET ACCUM = 15
             LHLD       SUBTTL       ;SET H,L PAIR → "SUBTTL"
             ADD        M            ;ADD ACCUM (15) TO MEMORY AT
                                     ; LOCATION "SUBTTL"
9-3.   (a)   INR        B;
       (b)   DCR        A;
       (c)   LHLD       TKSLFT;
             DCR        M
       (d)   INX        H
```

Chapter 12

```
12.2.  (b)   IF020:                  ;START OF IF ... THEN ... ELSE
                                     ; BLOCK
```

163

```
            CMP B                 ;TEST FOR ACCUM NOT EQUAL B
            JNZ THN020            ;
            JZ ELS020             ;
        THN020:                   ;DO IF CONDITION TRUE
            CALL SUBRA            ;
            JMP END020            ;THEN EXIT BLOCK
        ELS020:                   ;DO IF CONDITION FALSE
            CALL SUBRB            ;
        END020:
(d)     IF040:                    ;START OF CONTROL BLOCK
            CMP B                 ;TEST FOR B LESS THAN ACCUM
            JNC AND040            ;COMPOSITE BRANCHING FOR
                                  ; LESS THAN
            JC ELS040             ;
        AND040:                   ;
            JNZ THN040            ;
            JZ ELS040             ;
        THN040:                   ;DO IF CONDITION TRUE
            CALL SUBRA            ;
            JMP END040            ;THEN EXIT BLOCK
        ELS040:                   ;DO IF CONDITION FALSE
            CALL SUBRB            ;
        END040:                   ;THEN EXIT BLOCK
```

Index

About the Author

Ronald C. Turner received the Ph.D. degree (romance linguistics) from Harvard University in 1966. His field of specialization was acoustic phonetics. While at Dartmouth College, he implemented one of the earliest computer-assisted instruction systems for teaching foreign languages, and at Whitworth College he developed a CAI author language that incorporated graphics and slide projection. He spent two postdoctoral years at Washington State University in research, study, and teaching in computer science. Dr. Turner's current research interests are speech synthesis and computer-based analysis of language style. He has published papers that apply information theory to stylistics, and he is the author of two textbooks in Spanish. He is currently a software systems specialist at American Sign & Indicator Corporation.